◆ *Holy Women of Russia* ◆

Holy Women
of Russia

*The Lives of Five Orthodox Women
Offer Spiritual Guidance
for Today*

Brenda Meehan

HarperSanFrancisco
A Division of HarperCollins*Publishers*

Grateful acknowledgment is made for permission to reprint excerpts from the following:
From *Russian Peasant Women,* edited by Beatrice Farnsworth and Lynne Viola. Copyright © 1992 by Oxford University Press, Inc. Reprinted by permission of the publisher. From *Abbess Thaisia, The Autobiography of a Spiritual Daughter of St. John of Kronstadt.* Reprinted with permission of St. Herman of Alaska Brotherhood Press. From *Church, Nation and State in Russia and Ukraine,* edited by Geoffrey A. Hosking, "The Authority of Holiness: Women Ascetics and Spiritual Elders in Nineteenth-Century Russia" by Brenda Meehan. From *Prayer Book,* copyright © 1960, 1986 by Holy Trinity Monastery, Jordanville, NY. From *The New English Bible* ©The Delegates of the Oxford University Press and The Syndics of the Cambridge University Press 1961, 1970. Reprinted by permission.

FIRST EDITION

Library of Congress Cataloging-in-Publication Data
Meehan, Brenda.
  Holy women of Russia / Brenda Meehan. –1st ed.
  p. cm.
  Includes bibliographical references and index.
  ISBN 0-06-065472-4
  1. Christian biography—Russia. 2. Women—Russia—Religious life—History—19th century. 3. Monasticism and religious orders for women, Orthodox Eastern—Russia—History—19th century. 4. Monastic and religious life of women—History. 5. Russkaia pravoslavnaia tserkov'—History—19th century. I. Title.
  BX596.M44 1993
  281.9'092'247—dc20
                                                    92-53919
                                                         CIP

93 94 95 96 97 98 ❖ HAD 10 9 8 7 6 5 4 3 2 1

This edition is printed on acid-free paper that meets the American National Standards Institute Z39.48 Standard.

◆

*For Megan and Karen
and to the memory of my grandmother,
Anna Lynch Raleigh*

◆

◆

Contents

◆

Acknowledgments

A book like this requires much research, both here and abroad, and much time for thinking, brooding, and writing. I am grateful for the generous financial support I have received throughout the making of this book from the Kennan Institute for Advanced Russian Studies, at the Wilson Center in Washington, which enabled me to undertake a semester's research there; the National Endowment for the Humanities, the National Humanities Center, and the University of Rochester, which funded a year of research and writing at the National Humanities Center in North Carolina; and the Academy of Sciences of the USSR and the International Research and Exchanges Board, which supported my research in St. Petersburg (then Leningrad) and Moscow in the spring of 1989.

I am particularly indebted, in the United States, to Edward Kasinec, director of the Slavonic Collection of the New York Public Library, and to the library staffs of the Library of Congress and St. Vladimir's Theological Seminary. In Russia, I benefited greatly from the generous help of archivists and historians at the Russian State Archive of Ancient Acts, the Central State Historical Archive of the City of Moscow, the Russian State Historical Archive in St. Petersburg, and the Central State Historical Archive of St. Petersburg. My special thanks to Galina Alekseevna Ippolitova and to Boris Vasil'evich Anan'ich for their invaluable help and warm friendship.

I am grateful to colleagues at the National Humanities Center, who commented on early sections of the manuscript, particularly

◆ *Acknowledgments* ◆

Stanley Chojnacki, Gloria Pinney, Jonathan Ocko, Nikita Pokrovsky, Melvin Richter, and Bertram Wyatt-Brown; and to John Westerhoff of Duke Divinity School.

Many friends offered moral support throughout this undertaking. Of these, I owe a special debt to Irina and Iurii Speranskii for their generous hospitality in Moscow and memorable outing to Borodino; to Christine Long for her incisive comments and warm encouragement of my work; and to Barbara Fisher, who has been a part of this book from its inception, offering criticism, invaluable insight, and the empathy of a fellow writer.

I want to take this occasion to thank my father, Ross Meehan, my sisters, Maura Winkler and Anne Merritt, and my brother, Jim Meehan, for their loving encouragement. My daughters also helped: Megan, with data coding, and Karen, with the bibliography; they both know what a joy and support they have been to me.

Finally, I would like to thank Morris Pierce, in the University of Rochester's history department, for his computer skills and statistical analysis; Helen Hull and Joyce Ostberg for their painstaking care in typing the manuscript; and Jean DeGroat for her many years of generous help.

The transliteration of Russian names follows the modified Library of Congress system, with the exception of those of famous writers such as Tolstoy and Dostoevsky. Thus, Alexandra is rendered Aleksandra, Thaisia as Taisiia. Dating follows the Old-Style Julian calendar, which in the nineteenth century lagged twelve days behind that of the West.

Introduction

I have had great difficulty writing this book. I am convinced now that it is because the women I am writing about—vibrant, spiritually intense women—didn't like the way I was originally telling their story, making it part of a dry, scholarly analysis of the rise of women's religious communities in nineteenth-century Russia. It had been my intention to analyze in tidy chapters various aspects of these communities, including their origins, statistical profiles of their founders, the economic resources and institutional structures of the communities, the socioeconomic characteristics of the members, and their cultural significance in pre-revolutionary Russia. But these women jumped up from the pages, refusing to be neatly contained within my chapters and within a framework that stressed the sociohistorical at the expense of the spiritual. They insisted that I listen to the inner stirrings of their hearts and take seriously the spiritual paths they had trod. And I think they also wanted to say that holiness and spirituality are timeless, and that although their tale is that of another time and culture, and comes packaged in the unfamiliar disciplines and practices of nineteenth-century Russian Orthodoxy, the striving for an openness to a deeper presence is something we can all know and experience.

Through the passionate life of the widow Tuchkova, who founded in mid-life a religious community of women and took the monastic name Mariia, we see how the spiritual disciplines of the religious life enabled her to overcome profound grief and anger, transforming them into a fierce love of neighbor. In the hermit Anastasiia, we see an intensity of ascetic practice shocking to modern sensibilities, but one that enabled her to experience mystical union with the divine and earned her a reputation for holiness and wisdom among a wide circle of disciples. The peasant woman Matrona Popova, orphaned as a child and deeply sensitive to the loneliness of the homeless and the spiritual pilgrims of this world, lived a life of such profound humility and compassion that her reputation spread to the capital city of St. Petersburg. Aleksandra Shmakova, raised in a noble family in that dazzling capital, preferred the quiet of a chapel to the whirl of a ballroom. Married at a young age and convinced of the transitoriness of earthly things, she founded, after the death of her husband and daughter, a religious community for poor women, who revered her for her quiet sobriety and charitable acts. And finally, the energetic Abbess Taisiia, a zealot of the spiritual and aesthetic upgrading of women's religious life, combined a pious nature with acute intellectual abilities, leaving behind a rare spiritual autobiography and a frequently reprinted set of instructions to young nuns that inspired a whole generation of women to the meaning of a dedicated life and the search for holiness.

The holy women of Russia, whose lives form the core of this book, lived and worshipped within the newly developing women's religious communities of nineteenth-century Russia that formed as a grassroots resistance to the government's efforts in the late eighteenth century to limit the number of monastic establishments within the empire. Between 1764 and the revolution of 1917, over two hundred and twenty such communities were formed, primarily at the initiative of women like the ones described in this book. Although they began as unofficial monastic communities, by the end of the nineteenth century many had become recognized as official monasteries by the church and state authorities.[1] The five women described here are by no means the extent of Russia's Orthodox holy women, who were diverse and vivid from the time of Russia's conversion to Christianity in the tenth century to the present. They do, however, aptly illuminate both the changing and the changeless quality of religious experience. On the one hand, their lives are time specific, showing us nuances of holiness and aspects of popular piety and grassroots initiative specific to the formation of women's religious communities in nineteenth-century Russia; on the other hand, they saw themselves as vessels of a changeless God and humble followers of an ancient, sacred path laid out by the apostles and the early saints.

I have called these women holy: holy in the ordinary sense of the word, meaning people leading devout and godly lives dedicated to the service of God. None of them is considered an official saint of the church, although a recent Orthodox publication referred to one, Abbess Taisiia, as a saint.[2] But these women were held up in their time as exemplars of the holy life, models of holiness deserving of imitation. And their stories speak to us even today, for as John Coleman has said of saints, they "invite us to conceptualize our lives in terms other than mastery, usefulness, autonomy and control."[3] These women believed, and shock us into believing, in a world in which virtue has meaning.

This book attempts to show both the sources and the qualities of their holiness and how each woman represented a particular aspect of Orthodox spirituality. Their differences reflected the individuality of life circumstances, spiritual gifts, and aspirations. But all shared certain basic beliefs that inspired their spirits and shaped their understanding of the meaning of life.

In accord with their Orthodox tradition, these women believed in a providential God who had sent Jesus to redeem the world through his death on the cross, thereby making real the possibility of eternal salvation. This God was a loving God, a God with whom these women could enter into a love relationship more powerful and consuming than any earthly bond, including marriage. They also felt wrapped in bonds of intimacy and love with Mary the Mother of God, the saints, and the holy ones who had gone before them. Thus, as Peter Brown has said, the "Christ-carrying" man or woman had a sense of resources lodged deep within, "the resilience of bonds of invisible friendship with invisible protectors and with the company of the righteous."[4] The living and the dead were linked in shared relatedness to the divine; past, present, and future had meaning, for they were providentially ordained; and the faithful drew sustenance from their sense of being anchored in tradition.

One of these shared traditions, a tradition still very much alive in nineteenth-century Russia though feared lost in our modern secular cultures, was the tradition of holiness—an ability to perceive it in others, to value it, and to work toward its attainment.[5] People could be viewed as holy because concepts of holiness, sanctity, and piety existed within their culture.

Piety was a particularly important aspect of Russian religious life. The pious person honored the sacred icons, observed the elaborate rituals and fasts of the Orthodox church, and gloried in the beauty and liturgical richness of its onion-domed churches and monasteries. Along with piety, the virtues of humility and compassion were also revered. Indeed, humility was so privileged within Russian spirituality that it was seen as "the fundamental quality of the holy soul." Humility made possible the other virtues of gentleness, simplicity, and kindness—that tender compassion (*umilenie*) honored by the Russians, which found expression in almsgiving, acts of charity, and the gift of tears.[6]

Although piety, humility, and compassion were spiritual ideals for all Russians, monasticism, asceticism, and mysticism were chosen by only the few. Orthodoxy—unlike Protestantism or post-Reformation Catholicism—has continued to privilege the monastic or "angelic" life as a more perfect path to salvation. Maintaining the radical otherworldliness of early Christianity, the monastic ideal extolls a fleeing from the world, with its temptations and transitoriness, to concentrate on the "one thing needful," eternal salvation. As St. Serafim of Sarov (1749–1833), one of the great exemplars of the contemplative revival in Russia, explained:

> It is better for us to despise what is not ours, i.e., the temporal and passing, and desire our own, i.e., incorruption and immortality. For when we shall be incorruptible and immortal, . . . we shall be joined in a union with God surpassing the mind, like the heavenly minds. For we shall be like the angels, and sons of God, "being the sons of the resurrection" (Lk 20:36).[7]

The women of this book, women of nineteenth- and early twentieth-century Russia, all shared the belief of Russian Orthodoxy, the dominant religion of their culture, that the surest path to Christian salvation lay in the monastic life. Yet only one of them at an early age envisioned such a life for herself, and all of them encountered considerable obstacles and surprising turns in their lives before ultimately finding themselves following a monastic discipline. Rich and poor, middle-aged and young, who among them would have guessed that out of the pain at the loss of a cherished husband and child, or the boredom of aristocratic social life, or the shattering power of a mystic vision, or the simple but incorrigible habit of giving shelter for the night to the homeless, would slowly come that jarring, life-disturbing call to abandon oneself to God and take up the monastic life. Abbess Taisiia explained her call to monasticism as a heavenly fire enflamed within her, a divine spark that created a craving for solitude: "The more strongly this spark is enflamed, the stronger is the need to free the soul from the snares that enmesh it in worldly life, and to give oneself up to solitude for unimpeded attention to the one necessary thing (Lk 10:42)."[8] Monasticism fulfills the desire for Christian perfection and, as John Henry Newman has said, "will always be attempted by the more serious and anxious part of the community."[9] The monastic way of life, with its living traditions and time-honored disciplines, reflects a part of Christianity that is both eager for holiness and creative of it.

The women we are studying sought environments conducive to holiness and helped to create and shape those environments. They craved both the solitude central to a contemplative life and a community of like-minded women to share the richness of liturgy, sacrament, and prayer. Together they fasted, together they broke bread. In the privacy of their cells they followed their personal prayer routines, mortifications, and study of holiness. The disciplines they practiced helped them transcend bleak, spiritually dry periods in their lives; those same disciplines brought them moments of great joy and inner peace.

Although sharing the common roots of Orthodox spirituality, each of the five women in this book embodies a particular aspect of that spirituality in a more intense, even extreme, form. In studying their lives, we can see virtues embodied, dark undersides redeemed, and strands of holiness that sometimes seem disturbingly overdeveloped at the expense of a balanced wholeness. And, indeed, it might be that the holy are those who develop a particular virtue to an unreasonable extreme, such as Mother Teresa's single-minded ministry to the poor of Calcutta.

Certain qualities of soul marked each of these women, including a thirst for silence and a deep inner listening. All were greatly influenced in their spiritual practice by the ascetic models of the early desert saints and by the Eastern church's emphasis on an embodied theology and spirituality. Rather than craving dry theological treatises, they sought living guides—people wise in the ways of the spirit—and they themselves eventually became spiritual guides to others. As the monks Callistus and Ignatius of Xanthopoulos had urged in the fourteenth century, they spared no effort "in trying to find a teacher and a guide . . . a man bearing the Spirit within him, leading a life corresponding to his words, lofty in vision of mind, humble in thought of himself, of good disposition in everything, and generally such as a teacher of Christ would be."[10] Such a spiritual guide was called in the Russian tradition a *starets*, or elder. Through the figure of Father Zossima in *The Brothers Karamazov*, Dostoevsky has made the *starets* a figure familiar to readers outside the Orthodox tradition, but few realize that women also acted as spiritual guides, as the examples of the women in this book amply testify.

Although the search for spiritual guides comes clothed throughout these pages in the vocabulary and tradition of Russian Orthodoxy, there is a universal aspect to this particular search for holiness. As Kenneth Leech has written recently:

> A closer look at the lives of holy men and women throughout the history of Christianity shows us that those who searched with great fervor for an intimate relationship with God always asked for guidance and direction. Those who searched for God in the Egyptian deserts many centuries ago, as well as those who search for him in Calcutta, Tokyo, or New York today, have in common the desire for someone who can guide them through the wilderness of inner and outer experience.[11]

This desire for a guide through the wilderness of inner and outer experience is more acute than ever, a need deeply embedded in both Christian and non-Christian religious traditions as well as in the hearts of all spiritually thirsty people.

What do the women of nineteenth-century Russia have to say to us today, different as we are in time, place, and spiritual imaging? For those of Christian background trying to live a contemplative life in the midst of the world, there is much from an earlier vision of spirituality that is translatable into everyday living, as books like Richard Foster's *Celebration of Discipline: The Path to Spiritual Growth*, Tilden Edwards's *Living Simply Through the Day*, and Evelyn Underhill's *The Spiritual Life* attest. For those with a deep but unspecified sense of the sacred, Bruce Davis's *Monastery Without Walls: Daily Life in the Silence* can form a bridge between the experiences of women like Anastasiia and Tuchkova and the monk or mystic in each of us.[12] In these women's lives, we can also discern issues of special concern to women's spirituality, such as the importance of community, relation with others, and service[13] as well as the issues of holiness, creativity, and religious tradition, which transcend gender, empowering both women and men.

These women, and the spiritual tradition they adhered to, knew, valued, and inculcated practices that intensified religious experience, including long periods of solitude; a community of like-minded people that shared a moral vision; communal worship and private, meditative prayer; a sense of sacred space; the stimulation of sight, sound, and smell through ritual, chant, and sweet-burning incense; guides who knew and lived the holy way; disciplines that provided tools for psychological and moral transformation; and a tradition of pilgrimage, with its radical opening to the new and the divine. Much of this is common to the great religious traditions, and much of this can be practiced by people of spirituality outside the established religions.

But as I write this, I recall the voices of the women whose stories I am telling, warning that none of this can be superficial, and none of it is easy. Their call to God was hardly a limp surrender, and they followed a difficult path. In fact, what I am struck with at the end of writing this book is the difficulty encountered by these women in following their inner voices and the discipline required of them to do so. As a scholar and a woman mindful of the importance of the inner life, I value these qualities in these women. And I have come also to admire their strength of will, their gutsiness, and the flesh-and-blood character of their holiness.

As Russia struggles today to recover its religious tradition, it is fitting that the story of her holy women be told and reclaimed. Vital figures in the contemplative revival of nineteenth-century Russia, the women of this book are apt examples of a tradition newly made fresh, a holiness reaching beyond time and place.

♦

A Historical Note
Women and Community

Why was it necessary to found women's religious communities in nineteenth-century Russia? And what did these communities offer women?

To answer the first question, it must be kept in mind that the regulation of religion by the state in Russia had long preceded the Bolshevik Revolution of 1917. Even under the Tsarist government—for reasons deeply entwined both with Russia's Byzantine Orthodox tradition, which stressed the power of the ruler over the church, and the peculiarities of Russian political culture, which emphasized centralization and regulation of all aspects of life—the church had often been under the thumb of the government. In the eighteenth century the process of control accelerated: first, Peter the Great (1689–1725) abolished the office of patriarch (the highest ecclesiastical position in the Orthodox church), created the Holy Synod, a quasi-bureaucratic department of state to govern church affairs, and demanded a greater usefulness on the part of the church to the state; then Catherine the Great (1762–1796) confiscated monastic properties.[1] According to a decree promulgated in 1764, all church estates and the serfs attached to them became the property of the state.[2] Feudal dues were rendered to the state, and part of the considerable income derived from these was returned to the church in the form of clerical salaries. Now that the state had to pay clerical salaries and fund ecclesiastical institutions, it vigorously eliminated "superfluous" clergy, churches, and monasteries. In 1762, 881 monasteries had existed in Russia (678 men's and 203 women's); the reform of 1764 reduced the number by more than half, collapsing the total to 385, with 318 men's monasteries and 67 women's.[3] A tight budget was assigned to those monasteries that survived the cuts, and only a specified number of monks or nuns could enter a given monastery. Thus by the end of the eighteenth century, the state had sharply curtailed the opportunity for monastic life for both men and women.

In addition, opportunities for entry into monastic life were limited by the very structures and traditions of Eastern monasticism. Because of the Orthodox reverence for the contemplative and solitary life, the communal aspect of monastic life was underdeveloped, with most Russian monasteries following a noncommunal (idiorhythmic), rather than a communal (cenobitic), pattern.[4] In practical terms, this meant that not only did monks and nuns have to pay a fee on entering the monastery (as was true in medieval Europe), but they also had to fend for themselves once inside the monastery's walls. Rather than living in communal dormitories, they typically lived in private cells, which they purchased on entering the monastery and considered their own property; on transferring to another monastery, they could sell or dismantle their cell. They were also responsible for their own housekeeping tasks, food purchases, and food preparation.[5] Under these circumstances, the prevailing ones at the time this story begins, poor women had very little chance of taking up the monastic life no matter how strong their call.

Something had to change: new religious communities had to be formed, even if unofficially or surreptitiously, and they had to be self-supporting and communally organized, which, as will be seen, served to make them both spiritually stronger and financially capable of admitting and supporting women of the lower classes.

Such religious communities, called *zhenskie obshchiny*, or women's communities, began to develop, albeit in a faltering and groping way, in the late eighteenth century. The first of these communities were formed by tenacious nuns of suppressed monasteries. Soon, however, pious lay women began to establish unofficial monastic communities on their estates. By the middle of the nineteenth century, women's religious communities were also being formed by clusters of poor women as well as by renowned holy men and women. The formation of these communities was encouraged by villages and towns, which wanted the spiritual benefits and social services increasingly associated with these communities. Between 1764 and 1917, over two hundred and twenty women's religious communities were established in Russia.[6] Over the course of time, the church hierarchy and the government lent their approval to the communities, coopting and legitimating their energy and spiritual vitality without straining the government budget by contributing financial support. Many of these informal communities were eventually transformed into official monasteries.

Women's monastic communities spread throughout rural Russia in the second half of the nineteenth century. Since these communities were self-supporting, primarily through the communal labor of the sisters, they could offer more women, and poorer women, a means of support and opportunity for a dedicated religious life than the traditional monasteries, which were constrained by tight state budgets.

In addition to spiritual development, women's monastic communities offered women an opportunity to develop their leadership abilities and to exercise considerable responsibility. Women managed and worked large agricultural properties. They ran schools, almshouses, and orphanages and supervised the feeding, housing, and religious life of the community. As one scholar has observed of these women-run institutions:

In these monasteries each nun had the opportunity to develop her own talent, whether in the household, in field work, in marketing or selling, in administration, in a handicraft or a skilled craft where icon painting and the embellishment of the church stood in the forefront. Architectural talent was also valued, even if it was rarely found.[7]

These monastic communities further empowered women by teaching many of them to read. Reading was important for the liturgy, the observance of canonical hours, the recitation of the Psalter, the absorption of edificatory readings (particularly from the early church fathers and the lives of the saints), and the work of running the community and the orphanage. The literacy rates of the peasant women in the Tvorozhkovo community, for example, were well over the national average. According to the census of 1897, only 21 percent of the entire population of the Russian Empire was literate.[8] In the territory of what is now the Russian Federation of the Commonwealth of Independent States, the average literacy rate among rural men was 39.5 percent and among rural women, 11 percent.[9] By contrast, archival records for the Tvorzhkovo monastery show that in 1897, 89 percent of peasant women could read, and 35 percent of them could read and write.[10]

Monastic communities also offered women opportunities for autonomy, self-development, and even advancement: 17 percent of the women holding the position of mother superior or abbess in the dioceses of Nizhegorod, Novgorod, Moscow, and Tambov in 1903 were of peasant origin.[11]

It is difficult to answer precisely the question of why Russian women entered monastic communities in record numbers during this period. Empowerment and advancement were goals—and concepts—that few women would have acknowledged. As we will see, salvation was their most commonly affirmed motivation. In addition, a secure haven free from the most gnawing pressures of poverty must have been a factor for many. And the quest for community, for the companionship of like-minded women, could have drawn spiritually devout women together.

Whatever their motivations, entry into monastic life represented an opportunity for women to assert the radical importance of their own destinies. Although they would have disclaimed any feminist goals, they did in their own way make considerable claims to autonomy by the simple insistence that their own salvation was of paramount importance, more important than the claims of family, marriage, or village. Christ's precept to "leave father and mother, and come follow me," supported this priority, and the developing women's religious communities of nineteenth-century Russia strove to make this priority a real possibility for all women, rich and poor.

◆1◆

Fierce Attachments
Margarita Tuchkova and the Borodino Community

There we lived soul to soul; it was not for nothing
that we called each other sister: if one grieved, we
all grieved; if one was happy, we were all happy.

T. Tolycheva,
Spaso-Borodinskii monastyr'

he transformative power of religious life in community in-fuses the biography of the Russian noblewoman Margarita Tuchkova (1781–1852). At the time of her death, she was revered for her charity, keen sensitivity to the grief-stricken, and passionate devotion to the sisters of the community she founded at Borodino, yet her earlier life was marked by periods of great tragedy, rage, and spiritual despondency. To understand how she turned numbing loss into deep compassion, widowhood into community, and a headstrong willfulness into spiritual strength, it is important to study the role in her life of relationship, monastic discipline, and a desperate turning to the divine.

Margarita Mikhailovna Tuchkova was born into a socially promi-nent Russian noble family, the Naryshkins; her mother came from the equally aristocratic Volkonskii family. Even as a young girl, Margarita demonstrated a passionate, intelligent, volatile nature, being a "real quick silver" in the words of her biographer.[1] She especially loved music and had a wonderful voice; she also relished reading and could sit enrapt in a book for hours. Zestful and sensitive, she felt best when she could throw herself into some all-consuming interest or project. Neither time nor grief diminished her intense energy, and even when she had become an elderly abbess enmeshed in responsibilities, her movements were quick and impetuous and her speech animated. She was tall and shapely and, though plain faced, had striking white skin and vivacious green eyes.[2]

Margarita had three brothers and four younger sisters, but she seems to have been her parents' favorite. They introduced her into society at the age of sixteen and soon arranged what they hoped would be a good marriage to a young nobleman with dazzling career prospects. Instead, he proved to be of shockingly dissolute character, in fact, the scandal of St. Petersburg, and a divorce had to be arranged. Deeply wounded, Margarita returned to her parents' home, still reeling from the psychological blow she had experienced. During this difficult time, Margarita met and fell in love with a handsome and sympathetic military officer, Aleksandr Alekseevich Tuchkov, a future hero of the Battle of Borodino. When her parents, fearful of another scandal, refused his offer of marriage, he took a trip abroad, hoping to distract himself. While abroad, he wrote her a poem, each stanza of which ended with the lines:

> Qui tient mon coeur et qui l'agite?
> C'est la charmante Marguérite.[3]

Years passed and their love endured. Finally, in 1806, at the age of twenty-five, Margarita received her parents' permission to marry; thus began an ecstatically happy though tragically short period of her life.

Margarita adored her husband, priding herself on his good looks and basking in his reputation for bravery and chivalry. Inseparable from him, she accompanied him on military campaigns, to the distress of her family and friends. During the Swedish campaign she developed a reputation for kindness among the soldiers and the poor and acted as a nurse to both the Swedish and Russian wounded.[4] In April 1811, to their indescribable joy, a son, Nikolai Aleksandrovich, was born to Margarita and Aleksandr; Margarita herself nursed him, an unusual thing for an aristocratic woman.

But their domestic bliss was soon to be blown to bits by the roaring guns of Napoleon's invading forces. Aleksandr, who had by then reached the rank of general, was dispatched with his regiment to the area west of Moscow to take part in the defense of "Holy Russia" against the advancing French army. On August 26, 1812, during the famous Battle of Borodino—a battle brilliantly depicted by Tolstoy in *War and Peace* and hauntingly commemorated by Tchaikovsky in *The 1812 Overture*—General Aleksandr Tuchkov died, along with forty-five thousand Russian and thirty thousand French officers and soldiers.[5]

On September 1, Margarita's name day, a military courier arrived to tell her the news of her husband's death; she fainted on hearing it. When she came to herself, she set out hurriedly for Borodino to find his body. The scene she found was not pretty: thousands of bodies stretched across an immense and unforgiving field, with the smell of decay already fouling the air. Margarita was waved away several times by those assigned the grim task of sorting the dead, but she was determined to find her husband and to know the spot where he had fallen. Obsessed with grief, she persuaded an old monk from the local monastery to help her find her husband, and to offer a *panakhida*, the Russian liturgy for the dead, over his remains. Though they searched through the night, they were unable to locate him. Finally, they came on a soldier who pointed out to Margarita the spot where her husband had fallen, grimly explaining that when General Tuchkov was first wounded he had lost his arms. The soldiers of his regiment had tried to carry him away when a second shell hit, blowing them all to pieces.[6] Beneath a nearby pine tree, she found his wedding ring.[7] Margarita would return to this spot again and again, eventually building a church there in honor of her husband. In the future, she would also build a women's religious community at this spot, although she could hardly foresee this event at such an intense moment of mourning.

Exhausted and horrified, Margarita returned to her estate in Tula, where she was watched over anxiously by her companion, Madame Bouvier, Nikolai's nanny. Her grief was so intense that Madame Bouvier worried not only for her beloved mistress's health, but even for her sanity. On occasion Margarita became delirious, believing that her husband had not been killed but taken captive. One chilly autumn night she was found wandering in the woods in a light muslin nightgown, searching for him with a lantern. Her mother-in-law (who herself had lost not only Aleksandr but also an older son, Nikolai, and whose other son, Pavel, had been taken prisoner) came to comfort Margarita and to play with her little grandson, Nikolai. At this point in her life, Margarita was more consoled by hearing her mother-in-law say how much her grandson resembled his father than by her soulful sighs of "God's will be done."

Margarita later described her mental state at this time in a letter to her son:

> I don't remember what happened to me when I heard the news; others can tell you this . . . I pray to my Saviour to forgive me my delirium. It reached such a point that when my mother spoke to me about the blessings of paradise and the rewards which await us if we know how to bear the cross which God sends us, I responded that I didn't want even paradise itself without my Aleksandr and no recompense existed for a soul annihilated by grief.

She went on to explain that about four months after the news of Aleksandr's death, she heard her son say one night in his sleep, "My God, give papa back to Nicky." She was so touched by his prayer that in her unbalanced state she began to see him as a saving angel, a being so heart-rendingly innocent that God, hearing Nikolai's prayers, would surely have to respond by returning his father to him. And so she lived in a state of blind hope for another year, only to collapse into greater despair when she finally had to admit to herself the tragic reality of his death.[8]

Slowly Margarita began to put her life together, moving from her isolated estate to Moscow. There she met Filaret (Drozdov), the future metropolitan (governing hierarch) of Moscow and friend of the Tuchkov family, who would later become her spiritual counselor. During this time Margarita developed the plan of building a church in honor of her husband on the spot where he had died. Determined, indefatigable, and well connected, she eventually received permission for the construction of the church and even a donation of ten thousand rubles from the tsar. But it was tough going in the beginning, and Margarita had to sell property and jewelry to realize her project. During the long years of construction, she traveled back and forth between the construction site and her town house in Moscow, where she was supervising the education of her son. While in Borodino, she lived in a modest lodge. In 1820 the church was dedicated, an elegantly simple, four-sided chapel of classical style, with unadorned white marble walls, a bronze iconostasis, and a marble cross with the inscription "Remember, O Lord, in Thy Kingdom, Aleksandr, killed in battle."[9]

One has the impression that the memory of his father, a memory constantly impressed on him by his mother, weighed heavily on Nikolai. On the occasion of his sixth birthday, on April 6, 1817, his mother wrote him a long letter in French telling him of her delight

21

in him, the happiness of her marriage, the bliss she and his father had felt at his birth, and the tragedy of their loss:

> Today you have turned six, my son. From this moment I will write down everything, everything that you say, everything that you do. I want to pass on to you the main traits of your childhood; you are already beginning to reason, to feel, and everything that you already say delights me—you are full of promise. May I, with the help of Divine Mercy, be able to instill in your heart all the virtues of your father. Your Father! At his name my entire being trembles. You do not know, my dear child, what you have lost in him and what your mother has been suffering since she lost that friend of her heart. You will see from our letters, which I have preserved as something precious, the whole history of our life; you will see how the feeling which united us one to the other was strengthened during our marriage; each year seemed to heighten our ties. . . . Your birth marked the height of our happiness. . . . How can I describe to you our joy at your birth? With your first cry I forgot all the suffering, all the fatigue which I had experienced while I carried you. In order not to be separated from your father, who had to accompany his regiment, I had endured the fatigue of a long march, and it was while on the road that I gave birth to you. At your birth everything was forgiven, we could only think of the happiness of having you, of loving you, of our loving each other all the more. . . .
>
> Shall I describe for you all the attention your father lavished on you in your infancy? As soon as he would return home, exhausted from his military work, he would run immediately to your cradle in order to rock you, or to pick you up and lay you on my bosom.
>
> With what rapture he gazed on us, and several times I saw tears of happiness in his eyes! But it was of short duration! You were only one year and four months when you lost your father.[10]

As this letter indicates, Nikolai was not allowed to forget his father or Margarita's devotion to his memory. One of Nikolai's earliest memories was of being brought to the Borodino battlefield and being shown the battery where his father had fought and heroically met his death; his mother handed him a small shovel and asked him to help her plant a poplar tree there in memory of his father.[11]

Margarita was as devoted to her son's upbringing as to her husband's memory. She soon buried her mother and her father and, with each new loss, became more attached to her son. In the words of her biographer, Nikolai became the "purpose of her life, her only happiness and her constant concern."[12] We can only imagine with alarm her sense of shock and utter despair when in 1826 Nikolai, at the age of fifteen and home for Easter vacation, suddenly took ill with scarlet fever and died within days.[13]

Margarita sank into a profound spiritual crisis. She tried to pray, but could not. She wandered back and forth from Moscow to Borodino, restless and unwilling to accept this second loss. She tried to understand why this tragedy had happened to her, what its meaning was. Devoid of inner peace, she tried to find peace in the faith of others and looked to people who had renounced the world for words of consolation or understanding. At Nikolai's funeral she had uttered, through her tears, the words of the prophet Isaiah: "See, I and the sons whom the Lord has given me" (Is 8:18).[14] The balance of this passage, a text known to Margarita, poignantly reflects the spiritual confusion and despondency she must have experienced after her son's death:

> See, I and the sons whom the Lord has given me
> are to be signs and portents in Israel,
> sent by the Lord of Hosts who dwells on Mount Zion.
> But men will say to you,
> 'Seek guidance of ghosts and familiar spirits,
> who squeak and gibber'
> a nation may surely seek guidance of its gods, of the
> dead on behalf of the living,
> for an oracle or a message?'
> They will surely say some such thing as this;
> but what they say is futile.
> So despondency and fear will come over them,
> and then, when they are afraid and fearful,
> they will turn against their king and their gods.

Then, whether they turn their gaze upwards or look
    down,
everywhere is distress and darkness inescapable,
constraint and gloom that cannot be avoided;
for there is no escape for an oppressed people.
                                        (Is 8:18–25)[15]

Feeling deeply oppressed by her suffering, Margarita continued to seek counsel and meaning from spiritually believing people. One of these was Filaret, metropolitan of Moscow, an austere but renowned church figure. One day when she went to see him, a woman with three sons was coming out of his office as Margarita was about to enter. After the woman had left, Filaret said to Margarita, "That was also a Borodino widow, with her orphans." "Three sons!" she replied bitterly, "while everything has been taken from me. Why?" He looked at her sternly and said, "Perhaps she has earned the mercy of God more than you through her submission." Stunned into silence, Margarita stood for a few minutes, then turned and ran down the stairs, leapt into her carriage, and returned home, whereupon she told her servants that she was not to be disturbed. After an hour, Filaret's black tandem pulled up, and he was able to convince a reluctant servant to announce him. When Margarita entered the room, he went up to her, saying, "I have offended you with my harsh words. I came here to ask your forgiveness." Thus began a deep friendship, one that was to have a great influence on Margarita.[16]

It seems clear that Filaret pointed out to Margarita, sometimes lovingly, sometimes firmly, what one source has called the "unChristian" character of her grief.[17] But we can only speculate on precisely what constituted this un-Christian aspect. Was it her non-acceptance of God's will, that absence of submission to the divine, of which Filaret had spoken? Was it her lack of faith, her despair, her inability to believe in the loving and providential nature of God? Was it her ego, inflated to the point of thinking that she alone had suffered great grief, that her sufferings were greater than anyone else's? How was it to be possible for this woman, a woman of flesh and blood, of will and rage and deep despondency, to transform herself and her life in such a way that she would eventually become a model for other women, a holy exemplar in the culture of her time?

Unfortunately, no sources clearly tell us exactly how she pulled herself out of her inner abyss, and there was certainly not an instantaneous transformation after her encounter with Filaret. But she did make the decision—whether because of his advice or because of something within herself—to settle down in Borodino, where she began the life of a pious, religiously observant widow. Her life began to center around the church she had built in memory of her husband, the Church of the Savior (Spaso-Borodinskii *khram*), and she started to follow a quasi-monastic routine of prayer and liturgy. In order to ensure daily liturgy, she established a trust of twenty thousand rubles, the income from which was to go to the Luzhenskii monastery in nearby Mozhaisk in exchange for which priests from the monastery would take turns offering the divine service in the church she had built. In the beginning, her life was very quiet: there were only she, Madame Bouvier, and an old servant living in the lodge. A few stray visitors would stay over from time to time, and an elderly widower, Gorlenko, having lost two sons at Borodino and become a monk after their death, had received permission from Margarita to settle in a hut on the edge of the church grounds. Margarita's routine was simple and repetitive. She arose early, dressed without the aid of a servant, and hurried to the church, where she sang in the choir stall. Writing to a friend at this period in her life, she reveals the simplicity and piety, as well as tedium and hope, of her daily routine:

> I can't report any details about myself—day follows day. Matins, Divine Service, then tea, a little reading, dinner, vespers, some small handiwork, and after a short prayer, the long night—this is all of life.

> It is boring to live, terrible to die—this is the subject for meditation.
> The Mercy of God, his love, here is my hope, thus will it end.[18]

It almost seems as though Margarita, knowing the value of piety in the Orthodox religion, was living a pious life, going through the form and the discipline, in the hope, and perhaps with the stirrings of faith, that if she offered herself bodily to God, she would eventually feel his love and peace. Margarita acted not only piously but also kindly. She offered shelter to those without a place to stay; she grieved with other widows who came to visit Borodino; she gave money to wandering beggars and the neighboring poor; and, as during the Swedish campaign, she took care of the sick. Word soon spread in the area around Borodino of "the good Noble Lady (*barynia*) who lives in God and loves her poor brethren."[19] A day rarely went by without some needy or sick person stopping by her sparsely furnished lodge, seeking alms, medicine, food, or comfort.

The church at Borodino began to attract other widows and mourners. Soon a small colony of women gathered around Margarita, who showed a particular empathy for people who, like herself, were wounded by grief or suffering. One day, when riding through a neighboring village, she came on a peasant driving a cart and heard a woman moaning in the back. Distressed by the sound, Margarita pulled alongside and inquired about the groaning woman. "A bitter lot has befallen her," explained the peasant. "She has two daughters, as stupid as they come, and her husband is bad. He is drunk from morning to night, and he beats all of them without pity. One time he terrified the little girls so much that they ran into the woods and spent the night there. May the Lord spare them from misfortune! But she, poor wretched one, took up begging as long as her strength lasted, but now has lost her arms and legs."[20] Margarita, appalled and perhaps recalling her own abuse at the hands of her first husband, was galvanized into action. She took the woman home with her, discovered that the daughters were indeed being beaten, persuaded the local authority who had jurisdiction over the mother and daughters to allow them to be transferred to Margarita's authority, and undertook responsibility for their care. She built for them a small lodging, and this shelter (a shelter, in effect, for battered women) formed the nucleus of the Spaso-Borodino women's community.

This community was composed of an odd assortment of women. A young peasant woman came from the local village to provide full-time care for the invalid mother. Soon this young woman was caring for other lame and elderly women, and a small almshouse was built. There were also women, both rich and poor, who wanted, as they said, "to leave the world" and live a life of prayer. Margarita gave these women permission to settle on the property she had acquired and become part of the developing community. Food had to be grown, a well had to be dug, a common kitchen had to be set up; through it all, Margarita bustled about in her black dress, supervising the work.[21] Savva, archbishop of Tver, later described the origins of the community: "Around Margarita Mikhailovna's cabin there began to be built cells of voluntary hermits, recluses from the world, part of them from gentry families and part from prosperous merchant families; added to them were poor widows and maidens who, ready for honorable work with prayer, took shelter there."[22] In the evenings, Margarita gathered this varied collection of women, many of whom were illiterate, around her to read to them, instruct them, and talk with them about their needs and spiritual longings. She soon became "*matushka*" (mother) to them all and thus began to re-create the family she had lost.

By 1833 the community had grown to over forty women.[23] It was an unofficial religious community, begun spontaneously and growing somewhat haphazardly but following a religious discipline of prayer and work. A choir had been formed, with Margarita herself giving singing lessons to the young women and a musician hired from Moscow to train choir members in the intricacies of Orthodox liturgical chant. Every August 26, an elaborate liturgy commemorated those who had died in the Battle of Borodino, followed by a large procession, which attracted people from miles around. The time had come, in the eyes of both Margarita and the church and government authorities, to regularize the community and give it official sanction.[24]

The community developed in a society structured by serfdom and chilled by the vehemently conservative policies of Nicholas I (1825–55). Having come to the throne only after quashing the Decembrist Revolt, a rebellion instigated by those favoring a Western democratic style of government and opposed to autocratic rule, Nicholas was profoundly suspicious of any sign of autonomous grassroots activity. Every aspect of society, including the church, had to be brought under the purview of the central authorities.[25] Thus, an independent religious community of lay women, pious though it might be, warranted investigation and supervision by the Holy Synod, the governing body of the Orthodox church and administrative arm of the central authority.

In 1833 the Synod began the process of officially "establishing" the community at Borodino as a *zhenskaia obshchina*, or women's religious community. The process, which subsequently was to be used in officially sanctioning other freely formed communities of women, involved an elaborate investigation of the financial resources of the community, to assure the Synod that the community would be self-supporting; the social and juridical status of the members of the community, to ensure that there were no runaway serfs or others lacking the legal right to settle there; and the moral probity and religious rule by which the members of the community would live.

To prepare for the official recognition of the community of women at Borodino as a *zhenskaia obshchina*, Margarita had to settle her financial affairs and pledge her assets to the support of the community. She freed the serfs on her Tula estate, an unusual thing for her time.[26] In return for the use of her land, the freed peasants were to pay her an income of two thousand rubles each year, which she pledged to the community. In addition, she sold half of her Iaroslavl estate for twenty thousand rubles, the income from which was to go to the community, and she allocated her widow's pension to its support.[27]

Since the more elaborate rules and charters for women's religious communities were worked out in the 1840s and 1850s, we do not have a clear sense of the juridical status of the members of the newly recognized Spaso-Borodinskaia *zhenskaia obshchina* or the religious rule they followed, although we do know that the sisters followed a monastic routine as closely as they could and took turns in the perpetual reading of the Psalter in honor of the dead, a practice that continued until the revolution of 1917.[28] Margarita was recognized as the head of the community, the mother superior, and the other women were called sisters; they did not take permanent religious vows but pledged to be chaste while living in the community and to take part in its religious and work disciplines. Together they were groping their way toward a new model of religious institution—the autonomously initiated, self-supporting, and communally organized women's religious community, a form that would flourish in the middle and late nineteenth century.

One of the striking things about this new form of religious community was its ability and eagerness to support poor women, thus providing them an opportunity to lead the dedicated religious life. Although the Spaso-Borodino community was not wealthy, Margarita managed it extremely well and because of her efficiency, the sisters were rarely in need. The poor of the community received cloth, shoes, clothes, firewood, candles, soap, tea, and sugar. All of the sisters contributed to the support of the community through work. A farm and a cattle yard were set up on land donated to the community. In addition, the sisters practiced various crafts: they spun, wove, dyed flax and cloth, sewed cassocks and warm clothes, made shoes, bound books, and occupied themselves with painting the household and even icons. A refectory (*trapeza*) was built, where the sisters and Margarita ate simple, communal meals, mostly of bread and vegetables from the garden.[29] As the reputation of the community spread, generous benefactors also contributed to the community, including aristocrats such as Countess A. A. Orlova-Chesmensakaia, Princess T. V. Iusupova, and Count D. N. Shereme-tev and wealthy merchants such as Igumov, who sent a contribution of money and goods every year from Siberia.[30]

In 1837, on the twenty-fifth anniversary of the Battle of Borodino, an elaborate commemorative ceremony was held on the battlefield and was attended by Tsar Nicholas. Overwrought with memory and emotion, Margarita retired from the official ceremonies to her lodge, where the tsar afterward paid her a visit. Impressed by the orderli-ness and harmony of the community, he asked her if there was any way he could help her and the community. She thought for awhile and then replied nervously that the greatest kindness he could show her would be to free her brother, Mikhail Mikhailovich Naryshkin, from his banishment in Siberia, where he had been sent for partici-pating, as did many other young noblemen, in the Decembrist Re-volt. Taken by surprise, the tsar said that he would think about it; a few months later, Margarita's brother was released.[31]

Shortly after this, on a visit to Moscow, Margarita met with Met-ropolitan Filaret, who surprised her by suggesting that she become professed as a nun and that a petition be submitted to the Synod to have the Spaso-Borodino community elevated to the status of a monastery. He felt certain, he told her, that the Synod and the emperor would approve this. Margarita protested that she did not have the spiritual strength to be a nun. Filaret disagreed and urged her to give the matter serious thought, which she did.[32]

We do not know the inner workings of her soul, only that she was agitated by Filaret's proposal, prayed and brooded over it, and in the end decided to become a professed nun. At the same time, a petition was submitted to the Synod to change the Spaso-Borodino community to the higher ecclesiastical status of a monastery.

In 1838 the Synod approved the elevation of the community to a communal women's monastery. In 1840, on the Feast of the Apostles (June 28), Margarita was professed by Filaret in the great Trinity St. Sergius *lavra* (monastery) outside of Moscow. In the beautiful Orthodox tonsuring ceremony, in which the candidate for profession pledges to become the bride of Christ, Margarita uttered her vows with trembling voice and before the altar prostrated herself three times in three directions, representing the form of the cross. Filaret himself cut her hair and, to symbolize her beginning a new and angelic life, gave her the monastic name of Mariia. The ceremony was so touching, Mariia recalled in a characteristically emotional letter to the sisters of her community, that both she and Filaret were moved to tears, and it was only with difficulty that he was able to speak.[33] The next day, Filaret, who advocated restoring the position of deaconess, or consecrated widow, the ancient order of the early Christian church, consecrated Mariia both as abbess of the new monastery and as an Orthodox deaconess.[34]

Since the elevation of the community to a monastery entailed greater expenses (a permanent clergy, larger church, expanded living quarters and other communal structures) and a proof of the ability to be permanently self-sustaining, the resources of the community were again scrutinized by the Synod. This time Mariia pledged, in addition to the two-thousand-ruble annual income from her freed peasants and the income from the twenty-thousand-ruble note for the support of the clergy and liturgical and church needs, a fifteen-thousand-ruble note to go for the "maintenance of a common life" for the abbess and the sisters. In addition, she received uncommon permission from the Ministry of War to permanently pledge the eighteen-hundred-ruble-per-year pension she received as the widow of General Tuchkov to the support of the community.[35] The Synod approved the case for elevating the community to a women's monastery and passed it on to the tsar for his required approval. The tsar not only agreed but also, having been so impressed by the community during his visit in 1837, donated twenty-five thousand rubles for the construction of a brick wall around the monastery and a church with a refectory.[36]

Among the qualities that impressed people about the Spaso-Borodino community was its aura of harmony, a fact all the more remarkable given the great differences in social origin, education, and background of the women of the community. Although there is no specific document that outlines the social origins of the members of the community during Mariia's lifetime, we can glean from a variety of sources that there was a real mixture of women, including women from the gentry, the merchant class, the lower classes (tax-paying people), and from the clerical estate.[37] Highly cultured gentry women, moderately educated merchant women, and illiterate peasant women lived, worked, and prayed side by side, often teaching each other reading and the skills and crafts each knew. In addition, there were considerable differences in spiritual and moral characteristics, which stemmed as much from personality and religious experience as from class.

Spaso-Borodino had both a communal structure and a familial atmosphere. With all the intensity of her being, Mariia threw herself into the role and the reality of acting as mother to the sisters of the community, her newfound family. Just as she had done with her husband and her son, so she now became fully absorbed in the lives and needs of those she considered her spiritual daughters. Her letters exude a fierce love and attachment to her sisters. When she was away from them, she sent them her most heartfelt love; when one of them was gone, she keenly felt her absence. Like an anxious mother, she took on herself their worries, temptations, and sufferings. She responded to one of her sisters, who was away and had written to her about the spiritual anguish she was suffering, "May I dare to express my feelings in the words of the Apostle: verily, if one of you is sorely burdened, I am burdened with you."[38] To another sister, who was sick and had gone to Moscow to see a doctor and was alarmed at the prospective cost of her treatment, Mariia immediately sent money and a reassuring note, though she chided her for not having "learned long ago that what is mine is yours." She reassured this sister again in another letter, saying, "You know that I am yours, that I belong entirely to you, that I love you. When you comprehend all of this, you will be calm."[39]

Fiercely loving of her sisters, Mariia's manner of relating to them was forbearing, even permissive. Although she was an energetic and forceful administrator and oversaw major building campaigns for the monastery, she was criticized more than once for being an insufficient disciplinarian. Although she demanded strict adherence to the prayer discipline, she permitted innocent pleasures and conversations, and in one letter reveals herself as chiding rather than punishing a new sister for avoiding the communal refectory.[40] When faulted for her excessive indulgence of the sisters, she stressed the importance of love, answering:

> To the extent that we love the Superior of a cloister, to that extent is he helpful. His severity does not reform anyone, but hardens and

teaches cunning and lying. Sin finds its forgiveness in God, but evil and hatred estrange a person from Him, and woe to him who inspires these in another.[41]

The communal and the familial nature of the monastery impressed both the sisters and visitors. A communally organized monastery was still the exception in Russia, a culture wherein the idiorhythmic monastic pattern, with its unnerving fend-for-yourself ethos, still dominated. Although Archbishop Savva believed that during the earliest stages of the Borodino community there were "hermits and workers" and that the hermits, being more prosperous, had built their own cells, over time the communal character of the monastery solidified.[42] Communal living quarters and a refectory were built, the haphazard cells of the hermits began to disappear, and a common life of prayer and work emerged, though the nature of the work may have varied according to the social origins and skills of the sisters. In contrast to the traditional idiorhythmic monasteries, at Spaso-Borodino "each served the other with work appropriate to her abilities, and it was severely forbidden to accept payment one from the other." According to one observer:

> The Mother Superior molded a Christian community in the full sense of the word. The number of monastics reached up to 200, and there is no doubt that not all among them were deserving of esteem, but the general spirit of the cloister reminded one of the time of the early Christians. Borodino nuns who have now settled in other monasteries, were for a long time unable to get accustomed to their new way of life, as I happened to hear from several of them. Among others, one of them told me: "There we lived soul to soul; it was not for nothing that we called each other sister; if one grieved, we all grieved; if one was happy, we were all happy. But here everyone is on her own. How can we serve each other if we agree about the price—that is outrageous to us."[43]

When Mariia died in 1852 at age seventy-one, Filaret wrote to the Synod explaining the necessity of picking her successor from among the women living in the community, rather than from another monastery, because of the "communal character of Spaso-Borodino."[44] As part of the process of interviewing the nuns of the monastery about a successor, he inquired about the style of Mariia's rule. One of the nuns, Sofiia, expressed to him "esteem for her memory, for her many good works, although she recognizes that because of her kindness there wasn't sufficient strictness." Filaret concluded that this remark was "not insulting and not unfair" to Mariia.[45] One of Mariia's laxities, which Filaret learned to his dismay when her successor, Abbess Sergiia (who was also of noble background and had buried a husband and son at the Borodino monastery cemetery), started sorting through the paperwork of the monastery, was to have soft-heartedly accepted some women into the community without sufficiently checking their internal passports and registering them with the appropriate authorities. Although troubled by this, Filaret wrote to Sergiia, reminding her that "Mariia had built the monastery from scratch, and according to methods peculiar to her, and that under these circumstances she had a few rights to indulgence, even if she acted more capriciously than was strictly legal." He admonished Sergiia, however, that now that the monastery was well established and no special circumstances existed, there was no excuse for a weak observance of the prescribed regulations.[46]

Mariia had, in fact, acted pretty much as she wanted in the governing of the Borodino community, and the impression left of her is of a woman of great residual willfulness. It was will and determination that had enabled her to build a memorial church, a women's community, and a flourishing monastery. Once committed to someone or something, Mariia used every personal resource and every powerful connection she had—and she had many—to help that person or plan prosper. She had used her clout to get the battered mother and daughters, though crown peasants, released into her custody, just as she had used some sort of power to gain access to her widow's pension.[47]

She seems to have had both presence and warmth. Heads turned when she entered a room, and despite her simple black *kamilovka* (nun's cap) and mantle, "she preserved up to the end of her life a certain type, which is equally appealing in young women and in old, the type which the French call 'la femme distinguée.'"[48] Whether in an infirmary ward or an aristocratic salon, her lively voice and shining eyes drew people in, and there was an appealing intensity in her manner.

To her own distress, Mariia bore the marks of her class background, refined upbringing, and acute sensibility to the end of her life. Although she treated those who turned to her for help with dignity and caring, she at times inwardly winced at her own squeamishness and fastidiousness. When someone arrived suddenly at her door with a festering sore to be treated or dirty bandages to be changed or a bloody wound to be sutured, she responded compassionately and effectively, but no sooner had they left than she scrupulously washed her hands and threw herself on her cot, feeling faint. When ragged peasants, particularly one seedy old man from the local village, would stop by in the cold of winter for a cup of tea or tumbler of hot rum and, rank with the smell of sweat and tar, turn to her for advice and comfort, she would respond kindly and then afterward air out the room or even sprinkle about eau de cologne. Ashamed of this reaction, she said on one such occasion to her cell assistant, "You see how worthless I am. These poor ones turn to me from the goodness of their heart, and love me, and I am capable of being disgusted by them!"[49]

Another of Mariia's troubling traits was her almost morbid preoccupation with the memory of her husband and son. More than the faithful widow of biblical esteem, Mariia clung to the graves of her dear ones, cherished her mementoes of them, and sat brooding for long periods of time under the poplar tree she and Nikolai had planted. One time, years after Nikolai's death, she fell into such an emotional state while visiting his crypt that the sisters found her lying there unconscious. Informed of this, Filaret forbade her to visit the crypt and ordered her to throw out all of Nikolai's toys and trinkets she kept on a shelf in her room. Incapable of doing this, she hid his treasures in a trunk and looked at them wistfully and clandestinely from time to time.[50] How, then, to sum up this very real woman—willful, squeamish, passionately attached to her community, and indelibly marked with grief? How did she become an exemplar for other women of her time and culture, and what qualities rendered her holy (*sviataia*), as some of the neighboring peasants called her after her death?[51]

Her outstanding characteristic was her generosity, her charity to the poor and the unfortunate. She was, as the neighboring peasants noted, the "good noble lady who lives in God and loves her poor brethren." Not only was she generous in almsgiving, as her Orthodox culture urged, but also she had renounced a life of luxury and shared what wealth she had with the women who settled around her, some poor, some homeless, some widowed, some young.

She was also known for her compassion, her special empathy for those who suffered and grieved. The root of her intense connection with other people lay in her sorrowing heart, which sensed the grief of others and understood that suffering felled the rich and the poor alike.

The fervor of her love for others was palpable and contagious. The sisters of the community felt it daily, and she stressed the importance of love by instruction and by example. Over the entrance to the communal dining hall, itself a symbol of Christian *agape*, she had had inscribed her two favorite exhortations from the Bible. The first, from Paul's first letter to the Corinthians, read: "And though I bestow all my goods to feed the poor, and though I give my body to be burned, and have not charity, it profiteth me nothing" (1 Cor 13:3). The second, from an epistle of St. Peter, read: "Seeing you have purified your souls in obeying the truth through the spirit unto unfeigned love of the brethren, see that ye love one another with a pure heart fervently" (1 Pt 1:22).[52] One can hardly imagine a more emblematic statement of Mariia's life and manner of relating to other people than this: love one another with a pure heart fervently.

Fervent bonds of love and intimacy bound the sisters of the community to each other and to Mariia, whom they called their dear mother. We are told that at Mariia's funeral, the grief of the sisters was so acute that they could not continue singing, and her burial had to be completed without the customary choral chant.[53] And when Abbess Sergiia attempted to introduce reforms into the monastery after Mariia's death, Filaret warned her to do it in a way that would not tarnish the memory of her predecessor, because the sisters had dearly loved Mariia.[54] Somehow Mariia had managed to maintain the feeling of intimacy of relationship within the community, despite its growth to over two hundred sisters at the time of her death in 1852.

Abbess Mariia left behind her a successful community, one that became a model both for its manner of founding and for its communal and democratic (socially diverse) organization. Although she was not the first widow to form a *zhenskaia obshchina* (Princess Evdokiia Meshcherskaia did so on her estate in Anosino in 1821, following the death of her husband and daughter[55]), Mariia's community at Borodino was particularly renowned and inspired other women to think of forming religious communities on their estates. Thus, Anna Gavrilovna Golovina dreamed after the death of her husband of building on the ancient Golovin estate of Novospasskoe, a women's community modeled after that of Spaso-Borodino. With the acquiescence of her son, she carried out this plan, and in 1852 the community, known as Spaso-Vlakhernskaia, was officially recognized by state and ecclesiastical authorities.[56] In the course of the nineteenth century, widows of all social classes—not just aristocratic women—participated in such endeavors, and over twenty communities were formed by them.[57]

In inspiring other women to live simple and spiritually focused lives on their estates; to share their property; to live among and, in many ways, as peasants; and to be anxious to teach other women, Margarita Tuchkova prefigured by half a century aspects of the great Russian novelist Leo Tolstoy's spiritual vision for his life of simplicity and work among the peasants at his estate of Yasnaya Polyana. The opportunity she created through the Borodino monastery for women of all classes to lead dedicated religious lives endured beyond her death until the revolution of 1917. During her lifetime, many of the women she attracted to the Borodino community were from the lower classes. After her death and following the emancipation of the serfs in 1861, peasant women undoubtedly formed an even larger proportion of the Borodino monastery. In 1911 the monastery had 265 *desiatiny* of land (715 acres), with the sisters themselves working the fields. The monastery included a parish school for thirty girls, a small hospital, and an almshouse for elderly sisters. In addition to the abbess, there were fifty professed sisters and 195 novices (*poslushnitsy*).[58] According to a document found in the archives of the diocese of Moscow, there were in 1914 fifty professed nuns in the Spaso-Borodino monastery, thirty-three of whom were of peasant origin, thirteen from the lower artisan class (*meshchanstvo*), two from the nobility, one from the merchant class, and one from the clerical estate. The abbess was of artisan background, and the treasurer was of peasant origin.[59] Thus, Margarita had created an institution that not only supported women of the lower classes in their religious aspirations, but also offered them considerable opportunity for the development and exercise of their abilities.

The Borodino community bore the stamp of Margarita's intense personality. As far as is known, Margarita's entry into religious life was not so much marked by a radical transformation of personality (such as loss of will, ego, or attachment) as by the creation of a new forum for her energy and a new object for her attachment. Perhaps because she had never undergone the rigorous training in obedience and submission of will associated with the standard novitiate of an Orthodox monastic, her personality and will remained vividly intact. In her, holiness and impassioned character were two readings of the same text.

♦ 2 ♦

A Jarring Translucence
Anastasiia Logacheva, Hermit and Staritsa

> What religion reports, you must remember, always
> purports to be a fact of experience: the divine is ac-
> tually present, religion says, and between it and our-
> selves relations of give and take are actual.
>
> > William James,
> > *The Varieties of Religious Experience.*

I f this were a fairy tale, it could easily begin with the familiar opening: "Once upon a time, in the deepest part of
the forest . . . ," for it was in the deep forests of Russia that
Anastasiia Logacheva (1809–75), a renowned ascetic and holy
woman, spent the most intense periods of her life. Like many mystics, she lived in two time zones, the present and the eternal. In the
present and the temporal, she was a humble peasant woman subject
to the usual constraints of her gender and class. In the eternal, she
experienced mystical union with the divine and radiated a charismatic authority that drew followers—rich and poor, male and female—to her. After her death, a monastic community formed in her
honor in the densely wooded spot where she had lived a life of radical solitude and wholeness.

Her story begins in the village of Kudlei in the heavily wooded Ardatov district of Nizhegorod province in central Russia. There, in 1809, she was born to peasant parents. At the age of eight, she suffered an emotional blow when her father was drafted into the army. He soon after called for her mother and younger sister to join him, leaving Anastasiia, feeling abandoned, to the care of her paternal grandparents and her uncle and his large family. The years ahead loomed bleak and long, since at that time the term of service for a peasant conscripted into the tsarist army could last up to twenty-five years. Whenever Anastasiia felt particularly lonely, neglected, or misused in her relatives' crowded and demanding household, she would run to the barn and, with tears in her eyes, pray to the Mother of God for comfort, as her own mother had urged her when she kissed her good-bye. Her natural quietness deepened into a strong yearning for prayer and a solitary life. From the age of twelve, she began to shun even the most innocent games with her friends, who, to their astonishment, would often come on her in a ravine or a field, her arms outstretched to heaven, enrapt in prayer; at other times she would walk with them for awhile, and then suddenly disappear into church as though she found their chatter unsettling. She frequently went with her grandfather into the woods, where he kept a beehive. There, in a quiet place along a ravine, she dug a cave in the hillside, where she spent as much time as she could steal from her errands at home in prayer and fasting. Her desire for solitude and prayer grew stronger each day. Alone in these longings, she craved support from someone who had experienced similar yearnings. When she heard of the highly ascetic life of Serafim of Sarov (1759–1833; canonized 1903), she set out at the age of seventeen for the Sarov monastery, which was about fifteen miles away. It was her intention to ask his blessing on her undertaking the life of a hermit.[1]

Anastasiia first saw Serafim in about 1826, and he was already an old man, with a flowing gray beard and a bad stoop from a beating he had received from thieves many years before while living alone in his isolated hut. For most of his adult life, Serafim had lived a life of dedicated solitude in the woods beyond the Sarov monastery, mindful of the dedication to prayer and discipline of the early Christian mystics who had sought salvation in the wilderness. For over eight years, he had lived in total silence, emptying himself of distractions to be open to the warmth of God's love and to sudden mystic visions of the Mother of God. Believing that in silence one could best heed the inner spirit, Serafim quoted St. Ambrose of Milan: "I have seen many being saved by silence, but not one by talkativeness."[2] In Serafim's experience, silence and prayerful meditation filled the soul with a godly warmth and peace. He described it thus:

> God is a fire that warms and kindles the heart and inward parts. And so, if we feel in our heart coldness, which is from the devil,—for the devil is cold—then let us call upon the Lord, and He will come and warm our hearts with perfect love not only for Him, but for our neighbor as well.[3]

To maintain this feeling of inner warmth, Serafim recommended to his disciples that they pray ceaselessly. He urged them to make the Jesus prayer an inseparable part of their lives, breathing rhythmically while repeating constantly the words "Lord Jesus Christ, be merciful to me a sinner." He instructed his listeners, "Walking and sitting, working and standing in church, coming and going, let this unending cry be on thy lips and thy hearts,"and promised them that when the prayer had become a ceaseless, unconscious repetition, they would find spiritual peace.[4] Serafim radiated an inner peace and joy, drawing disciples to him because of his magnetic holiness. In his later years, he ended his period of strict silence and took on the role of spiritual elder (*starets*), counseling those seeking his blessing, wisdom, or healing.

And so it was from Serafim that Anastasiia sought guidance and blessing. On the day she arrived at Sarov, she saw a crowd gathered in front of his cell, waiting for the renowned holy man to come out and greet them. Overcome with shyness, she stood at the back of the crowd and was startled when Serafim, having come limping out on his walking stick, looked at her directly, called her by name, and asked her to come close to him. Unable to utter a word, she drew close, and with a soul-piercing look, he said, "That which you are thinking about, that which you wish, the Heavenly Queen will bless, but the time has not yet come for it." And so she went back to Kudlei, patiently living her life of peasant work and prayer. After a year or two, she returned to Serafim to ask again for his blessing on her undertaking the life of a hermit. This time he advised her to go to Kiev, to the ancient Monastery of the Caves (as he himself had done at the age of seventeen, before undertaking monastic life) to seek guidance from "God's holy servants." On her journey to Kiev, she learned how to read from some pious peasant women who offered shelter to pilgrims.[5]

Shortly before Serafim's death in 1833, Anastasiia went for a third and final time to seek his blessing on a life of solitude in the woods. This time he blessed her intention, counseling her to settle in a spot where she could smell the fragrance of burning palms and to wear chains for the quieting of bodily desire. Between this visit, which occurred when she was about twenty-three, and her definitive undertaking of a life in the wilderness, almost seventeen years elapsed, probably because Serafim had also advised her not to leave her elderly parents, who had returned to Kudlei and were too old to work.

Particularly striking are her long years of obedience to Serafim of Sarov. Such obedience to a spiritual elder was an integral part of the

Orthodox spiritual tradition and was reinvigorated during the contemplative revival in Russia in the late eighteenth and the nineteenth centuries. Anastasiia accepted not only Serafim's general advice to wait until she was ready before undertaking a life of ascetic solitude, but also his specific admonition to fulfill her responsibility to her elderly parents before pursuing her spiritual inclinations. The necessity of fulfilling family responsibilities instead of dramatically casting them aside to seek a life in Christ seems to have been advice more commonly given to women than to men.[6] Anastasiia's situation is truly poignant: "abandoned" by her parents at the age of eight, she then must delay her vocation for almost twenty years while caring for her parents in their old age.

During her long years of waiting, Anastasiia supported herself and her parents by doing readings of the Psalter for the dead and by spinning and working in the fields. Her life was not anomalous, for Russian peasant society, being a religious culture, made room for the occasional pious single woman who wanted to lead a celibate life of prayer but who could not, for various reasons, enter a monastery. Such women were variously called *keleinitsy* (cell or hut dwellers, because their parents would often build them a separate hut on the outskirts of the village), or *chernichki* (from the Russian word for black, because they often dressed in black), or *spasennitsy* (those who wished to save themselves). As one nineteenth-century ethnographer reported:

> Frequently girls reject marriage and express the wish to "save themselves," to "leave the world." No matter how unpleasant for the parents, in most cases they do not feel they have the right to refuse her. In earlier times such *spasennitsy* went into monasteries; now since state monasteries have seriously diminished and entering a monastery requires an offering, often very large (100 rubles and more, for example, for the Sviatozerskii convent in Gorokhovetskii district), these *spasennitsy* rarely enter monasteries. More often, they

set themselves up in their own village or in the nearest village to be close to the church. Parents are obliged to build her a hut on the outskirts of the village. Sometimes she moves there with 3–5 *spasennitsy*.[7]

Anxious to read the church services, scriptures, and other devotional literature, such women were often literate. In addition to doing spinning, weaving, knitting, and day labor for prosperous peasants, these *spasennitsy* frequently earned income through the reading of the Psalter for the dead, an ancient Orthodox custom in which the Psalms—those majestic prayers of both the Jewish and Christian tradition—are read continuously over the body of the deceased for the forgiveness of the sins of the departed and the comfort of the bereaved. The Psalter is traditionally read on the fortieth day after burial and on the anniversary of the death. Thus, a pious and celibate woman like Anastasiia could serve an important role in the peasant village, where a priest was often unavailable or unwilling or too expensive for the time-consuming undertaking of reading of the Psalter. In 1900, a prominent professor at Khar'kov Ecclesiastical Seminary criticized the authority and reputation that pious women who performed the reading of the Psalter gained in the village as "women wise in the word of God" and advocated that male psalm readers take over this role.[8]

After the death of her parents, Anastasiia gave whatever she had to others and, at the age of forty-one, prepared for a life of solitude in the woods. After a pilgrimage to Murom, during which she suffered a near-death experience that lasted, symbolically, for three days, she returned home and then settled into a deep, impenetrable part of the forest to take up in earnest the life of a hermit. She called the spot Kurikha, because it had the fragrance of burning palms. Here the long-awaited ideal became a palpable, riveting reality. Bitterly cold in winter, stifling in summer, her hand-dug-out hut echoed with the howls of the wild animals that roamed the forest.

Bears and wolves were constantly present. When she attempted to plant rows of vegetables, she was discouraged to find that each evening they were torn up by a bear. She suffered from temptations and initially found it hard to concentrate on the life of an ascetic. But she persevered, following the disciplines of mind and body central to the ascetic tradition. Wishing to empty herself of bodily desire so that she might become a willing, open receptacle of God's grace, she disciplined her body through strict fasting, long prayer vigils, and severe ascetic feats. Her diet consisted primarily of root vegetables; she ate once a day, in the evening, in small portions. On one occasion, she observed a complete fast for forty days, while standing motionless on a rock in prayer, arms outstretched, making of her very body a sign of the cross. She slept rarely, often standing through the night in prayer or in the reading of the Gospels. Like her model, St. Serafim of Sarov, she read one gospel in its entirety every day, repeating the sequence over and over again throughout her life. She gloried in liturgical prayer and in the reading of the Psalms, *akafisty* (Orthodox hymns of praise to the saints), and the prayer rule of the Sarov hermitage; in addition, she constantly repeated the Jesus prayer.[9]

Her prayer life grew more intense and extreme. Enrapt in prayer, she had often seemed to depart from those around her; now her mystic trances increased. On one occasion, a peasant came on her in the woods and was startled by what he saw: a woman standing in the midst of an ant hill, covered from head to foot with ants and a multitude of flies (the weather was hot), with blood streaming down her face.[10] It is uncertain whether she took this position out of a deliberate ascetic discipline or was suddenly awestruck by a sense of the presence of God.

The strength and courage needed to lead such a life of solitude in the woods caused people to pause and wonder how Anastasiia had such fortitude. The Abbess Sofiia once asked her if she were not afraid to live alone in such a deserted place, to which Anastasiia replied, in her simple, faith-filled way, "What should I be frightened of? . . . Of wild beasts? Of demon enemies? What will they do to me? Are they really more powerful than Jesus Christ the Lord or His most pure Mother?"[11] A timid or doubting person might have reminded her that even Serafim was brutally beaten by thugs in his hermitage in Sarov, but Anastasiia's serenity had a way of dissipating such responses.

Through prayer, fasting, and mystic moments, Anastasiia's sense of time became transformed: she lived in the present and in the eternal. She talked to animals, and they began not to bother her vegetables. She abandoned herself to the will of God, believing that Christ had already made salvation possible. She modeled herself after Serafim of Sarov and the desert saints whom he had taken as his model. She took to heart the ideals of the desert mystics, which had first been lived by the great ascetics of Egypt and Syria in the third and fourth centuries. These early Christians believed that following Christ's redemption of the world, paradise was potentially here, and that by radically pursuing God's purpose, in body as well as in soul, they could live as innocent and unalienated a life as Adam and Eve had lived before the Fall. One Syrian scholar has explained the theology of the desert ideal thus:

> Christ as Second Adam had opened the gates of Paradise anew for those who were saved and promised their return to that state of grace lived by the First Adam and Eve before the Fall. To hasten the fulfillment of this event, the believer lived in its expectation and sought in every way possible not to contribute to the continuing existence of this earthly realm, for example, by the procreation of children.
>
> But even further, the Syrian understanding brought a literal living out of life in the eschatological Paradise, as prefigured by Adam and Eve. More than a matter of celibacy, this understanding led the believer to adopt a life of stark symbolism: living naked in the wilderness exposed to the elements, eating only raw fruit and herbs, dwelling among the wild beasts, and leading an unbroken life of

prayer. . . . The believer lived what the true eschatological reality promised. To live as if it had already come was to hasten its actual coming; but there was, too, a palpable sense that to live as if it had already come was to accomplish its actuality.[12]

Anastasiia, like other Russian mystics and ascetics, followed the desert ideal of Eastern Christianity, seeing in the forests of northern Russia the symbolic equivalent of the Egyptian and Syrian deserts and referring to a hermitage as a desert (*pustinia*). In the starkness of the wilderness, she confronted her inner self and, through constant prayer, lived in an attitude of open and earnest expectancy to the divine. Like many mystics, shamans, and saints, she had a profound sense of holy presence. As Dana Greene has written in her study of Evelyn Underhill, the twentieth-century interpreter of the mystic life: "Participation in the holy presence is the spiritual life. It is not separate from life itself but is a particular way of apprehending it. The spiritual life is the 'commerce' between a person and the holy presence—God—an exchange which can suffuse and take over all of life, radically transforming it as it gains control."[13]

Others observed this transformation in Anastasiia. Sensing in her a holiness and wisdom, men and women from the neighboring villages came to seek her prayers and advice. In her very withdrawal from the world, she became a magnet for the troubled and the searching, a source of wisdom, objectivity, and certitude in an uncertain world. As one of her contemporaries commented:

> The world doesn't love pious and good people, but sometimes it seeks out, marvels at the ascetic feats of, and seeks counsel from these very people, when they withdraw from the world. And so it was with Natas'iushka: people from the local settlements began to come to her, to seek her holy prayers, to seek her counsel in the difficulties of life, and for several to seek instruction in how to be saved and how to pray.[14]

Another source reports that "nobody went away from her without kind words, without edification or understanding, without a quenching of the hunger or the thirst of her visitors."[15] A holy exemplar, she taught by doing, emptying herself of the personal and the inconsequential until she achieved that "jarring translucence" so characteristic of the ascetic.[16] One of her earliest disciples, Kotova, reports that she spoke rarely and had a constant, angelic smile.[17]

Anastasiia's life of solitude was difficult. She cautioned Vasilii Andreev, a peasant from the village of Kudlei who wished to follow her example and live as a hermit, of the hardships of the ascetic life, warning him that "as difficult as it is to sit naked peacefully in an ant hill, that difficult is it to live in solitude." Despite her sober admonitions, three peasant women pleaded to be able to live near her and follow her example. Felling the trees themselves and lugging the heaviest timber across the ground with rope, they built a small wooden hut near her cave. Although small and dark, it had three windows and a stove. There they followed a formal prayer rule laid out by Anastasiia, and each, like their mentor, did some form of manual work or handicraft while inwardly and constantly repeating the Jesus prayer. But the severe life of an ascetic and the unforgiving Russian winter began to wear on them, and after several months they resettled in the Ardatov Pokrovskii convent.[18]

Nevertheless, the paradoxical situation continued: Anastasiia, a hermit living a life of prayerful solitude, attracted to herself others wishing to live as hermits. These seekers marveled at the intensity of Anastasiia in prayer, during which time tears of joy and compassion would roll down her cheeks, while she remained oblivious to those around her. They sensed in her a deeper spiritual reality and wanted to make it their own. As Evelyn Underhill wrote: "We most easily recognize spiritual reality when it is perceived transfiguring human character, and most easily attain it by sympathetic contagion." Underhill made frequent reference to the fact that the life of the spirit is not "taught" but "caught."[19] Similarly, Anastasiia's followers tried to catch her sense of the holy.

With time, Anastasiia's reputation as a *staritsa*, a revered spiritual elder, spread through the region, and the number of people seeking her counsel and wishing to imitate her way of life grew. Although maintaining her original cave and her severe solitary prayer vigils, Anastasiia decided it would be necessary to build a house for those wishing to live near her, which perhaps might be the foundation of a women's religious community. But she was soon advised that this would require the permission of the local crown authority, since the woods she had retired to were crown property. This led to an investigation by the local authorities, who, among other things, sought information from the peasants of Kudlei about Anastasiia and the proposed community. Some objected that if a community or monastery were built, forest land not only would be lost but also meadows and apiaries. It was one thing to tolerate a pious recluse and a few followers, but it was something else to have agricultural land threatened. Other villagers warned that Anastasiia was incapable of building a community, since "she was often out of her mind."[20] Thus, the same quality of mystical intensity the pious and zealous characterized as holy appeared to others as insanity. Such confusion about penitential ascetics is not unusual. A recent scholarly study of sainthood in Western Christendom observed: "To be sure not every devout penitent was a saint, and the faithful were uncertain whether their would-be hero was holy or mad."[21] In the end, not only was her request refused, but also she was told she would have to leave her hermitage.

Evicted from her chosen place of solitude, Anastasiia tried to create the spirit of silence in the very midst of the village of Kudlei. Near the church, she built a hut. In its cellar, she dug a grave, where she retired for prayer. In order not to be disturbed, she resorted to the ruse of letting it be known in the village that she had gone on a pilgrimage; then, she would lock the windows, have someone bolt the door from outside, and live as though in her beloved wilderness.

The desert, she came to realize, was an attitude, not a place—a radical yet inclusive privacy within which the here and now and the infinite met.

This private apprehension of the infinite, the source of love, inevitably led Anastasiia to a loving awareness of the needs and concerns of others. A prayerfully powerful person, she often offered her prayers on behalf of others. At one point, when her cousin Pavel hanged himself in a drunken fit, she prayed and fasted for forty days for the lightening of his eternal fate. During this time she sought the counsel of another *staritsa*, the holy woman Pelagiia, on how forgiveness could best be obtained for her cousin.[22] While living in her cell in Kudlei, Anastasiia developed a passionate urge to go on a pilgrimage to the Holy Land. Reading the Gospels every day, she was steeped in the Jesus story and wanted to walk the paths Christ had trod, to rejoice at Bethlehem and grieve at Golgotha. She set out for St. Petersburg, where she boarded a ship for Jerusalem. It happened that several members of the royal family, including the grand princes, and government dignitaries were on board. During the journey, she became acquainted with a prominent government official to whom she gradually spoke about her life as a hermit at Kurikha, her desire to open a women's community there, and her difficulty in obtaining permission. The official suggested that she think instead of opening a women's community in Siberia, presumably because of the dearth of monasteries and religious communities in that distant area.[23]

When she returned from her nine-month journey, she attempted to resume her life as a hermit in Kurikha but was again driven out. Discouraged, she took up residence at the Ardatov convent. Her hut in the forest of Kudlei was dismantled, but the cellar and her coffin in the hut near the church in Kudlei, the site of many of her ascetic feats, remained. After her death, a chapel was built over it in honor of her holy austerity.

Her life at the Ardatov monastery was difficult. Having lived a solitary life for years, she found it painful adjusting to a cellmate, particularly one with the idiosyncrasies of the young novice Vera, who was assigned to live with her. Vera, for example, insisted on doing the laundry in the icon corner of their cell, a sacred space usually reserved for prayer, icons, and votive candles. A hundred times a day, Vera unconsciously assaulted Anastasiia's sensibilities until she became so distressed that she prayed to God to deliver her from this upsetting person. Then, aware of the sinfulness of this wish, she became literally sick with guilt. She undertook a strict penitential fast and prayed for forgiveness. During vespers one evening, she suddenly had a vision of the Mother of God, who appeared to her in radiant light, assuring her that her sins had been forgiven. Her serenity restored, she made peace with Vera and later took her with her when she was appointed mother superior of a newly established women's religious community in Siberia. While at the Ardatov convent, Anastasiia became known for her prophetic insight and good counsel; she also earned a reputation for radical nonpossessiveness, giving away her last crumbs to those in need.[24]

Anastasiia's appointment in 1863 as head of the new Nikolaevskii women's community in the Altai mountain region of Siberia is intriguing. Her biographer has suggested that her decision to move might have been motivated by the advice of the important government official she met on the trip to Jerusalem.[25] Being an appointment to a different diocese, it was most probably initiated by the Holy Synod, the governing body of the Russian Orthodox Church in St. Petersburg, and approved by the local Nizhegorod diocese in which Anastasiia lived, rather than being initiated at the local level and approved by the central authorities. Since Anastasiia had no administrative experience, her appointment indicates that priority was given to her spiritual experience and ability to direct others in the paths of asceticism and prayer, priority thus being accorded charismatic qualities over institutional concerns.

Little is known of the nature of the Nikolaevskii community or of the character of Anastasiia's leadership there; her biographical sources simply relate that Anastasiia became a professed nun in Tomsk, the diocesan center for the Altai region of Central Asia. She was tonsured by the bishop on the opening of the community and took the monastic name of Afanasaiia. She served as mother superior for five years and lived in the community another eight years until her death in 1875.[26] Documents found in the Synod archives show that the community was founded at the initiative of newly baptized Altai women, with the backing of a local merchant, and found support at top levels in St. Petersburg because church and government leaders were interested in encouraging missionary activity in remote parts of the empire, particularly among non-Christian natives.[27]

To the natives of the Altai, who revered nature and things natural, the Christian practice of dedicated celibacy must have seemed particularly strange. Nevertheless, the requirement of celibacy was accepted both by those women wishing to join the community and by parents giving permission to their daughters to do so. In their petition of August 1861 to the bishop of Tomsk to establish a women's religious community in Ulala, a village in the Altai region, the newly baptized women explained that they ardently wanted to "dedicate ourselves to the service of God in a solitary and unmarried state, and according to the example of Russian women's communities" but had until recently lacked material resources and permission from the authorities. Now, however, the Mother of God had sent them a benefactor in the person of the merchant Afanasii Mal'kov, who had pledged to fund all the necessary buildings for the community and to pay for their support until they were able to "feed ourselves by the work of our own hands." They explained that, having been baptized at the Altai mission:

> We now mourn the blindness of our unbaptized relatives and we consider the chief goal of our community and the first act of our service to God to be helping the mission in the Christian instruction of people of the female sex newly converted from paganism, in all their needs from birth to the grave, and particularly to take under our care sick, homeless and orphaned women.

The petition was signed by ten women, including two widows. Attached to the petition was the collective permission of the parents of the younger women, which asserted, "Wishing for our female children spiritual salvation, of our free will we do permit them to enter an unmarried life and a communal monastic community and even to take up the monastic model." Three unbaptized fathers gave their permission, specifying that what they were agreeing to was their daughters' right to "enter an unmarried life," a phenomenon that must have mystified them.[28]

And so it was to instruct these eager women in the celibate and monastic life that Anastasiia was sent to the distant outpost of Ulala. An embodiment of the contemplative life, she instructed in the Eastern Orthodox manner, by holy example. She continued to live a rigorously ascetic life and to act as a spiritual counselor, guiding the women in the ways of the spirit. She was known to have the gift of tears (a mark of compassion and extreme openness to the divine) and the ability to foretell when something bad was about to occur. On her death, she was found to be wearing penitential chains under her simple garb, something Serafim had advised her to do almost fifty years before. The chains, a vivid reminder of her ascetic fidelity, were buried in the coffin with her.[29]

After her death, she was venerated in three ways. First, her grave at Nikolaevskii monastery became a place associated with healing, and pilgrims, as well as many of the sisters of the monastery, believed in the curative power of dirt from her grave mixed with water.[30] Second, a chapel dedicated to her was built over the cellar of her hut at Kudlei. Third, at the initiative of peasants from around Kurikha, and with permission of the tsar, who ceded thirteen and a half acres of land, an almshouse was opened after her death on the spot where she had lived as a hermit. In 1899 the almshouse was transformed into the Znamenskaia Kurikhinskaia women's religious community, which in the early twentieth century was home to a mother superior, two nuns, and seventy-three novices.[31] A large part of Anastasiia's reputation for holiness stemmed from her extreme asceticism. Through the ascetic life, through the renunciation of sexuality and bodily pleasure, the ascetic is able to achieve great inner discipline and the emptying of the self preparatory to an inflowing of the divine. Asceticism has been admired by all levels of Christian society, but it has different class nuances. The dramatic renunciations of wealth and pleasure by the well-to-do are often commented on, but of equal note is the voluntary asceticism of a man or woman born into the lower classes. Given the severity of the usual peasant life, fellow villagers marveled that someone such as Anastasiia would willingly seek out more austerity in what often was sacrifice made for the sake of others. Ascetic feats of fasting, unbroken prayer, and bodily discipline were admired much as athletic prowess is admired today. Despite her asceticism, the overall impression one has of Anastasiia is of a woman of great joy, a woman for whom the great hymns of praise of the Psalms were as intrinsic a part of her life as the rigor of ascetic discipline. Imagine the effect over a lifetime of saying the Psalms every day, of waking before dawn to recite the prayers for matins, for which a frequently assigned psalm is Psalm 63:

O God thou art my God, early will I seek thee,
my soul thirsteth for thee; my flesh also longeth
for thee,
in a barren and dry land where there is not water . . .

For thy loving kindness is better than life itself,
my lips shall praise thee . . .

Have I not remembered thee in my bed,
and thought upon thee when I was waking,
Because thou has been my helper;
therefore under the shadow of thy wings will I
rejoice.[32]

Anastasiia's holiness was reflected in her joy, her compassion, and her asceticism. Asceticism was an essential prerequisite for her role as *staritsa*, a revered spiritual elder. In a pioneering essay on the rise and function of the holy man in late antiquity, Peter Brown argued that the authority of holy people derives in part from ascetic discipline, giving them a reputation for spiritual prowess and also rendering them capable of dispassionate judgment. By standing outside the ties of family, sexuality, and economic interest, the holy person is in an objective position, which makes him or her the ideal mediator and counselor, first, for local villagers, and later, as reputation spreads, for city dwellers. The certitude and commitment of the ascetic's life appeal to those troubled by anxiety and uncertainty; through a life in the wilderness, the ascetic is frequently believed to have power over nature and animals. In a subsequent article, Brown has examined the bonds of love and esteem that bind the holy person as exemplar to disciples and clients.[33] In addition, the ascetic or the holy person has gained a wisdom and knowledge that others seek—the wisdom of knowing the value of simplicity and sparingness and the joy and serenity of contemplation and inwardness.[34]

As hermit, ascetic, and *staritsa*, Anastasiia embodied many of the qualities of the holy person described by Brown. Once Anastasiia withdrew from the world, leaving behind family and village ties and obligations, she was able to take up the life of a fully committed ascetic. As she emptied herself of bodily longings, she developed the translucent radiance of the true ascetic and the ability to calm animals. A radical transformation of personality, the goal of monastic and contemplative life, took place within Anastasiia, clearing her of attachments and petty strivings and making her a willing vessel of the divine, a mediator between the temporal and the infinite. She shone with an inner radiance that attracted followers to her even in the depths of the forest and led many to sense in her the power of a deeper reality. It was during the forest period that her reputation for holiness and wisdom grew, and she was sought out as mediator, model, counselor, and *staritsa*.

There are many paradoxical elements within Anastasiia's life. Her inability to found a community of her own at Kurikha, owing to charges of madness and her lack of control over property, shows her powerlessness within the social and legal system. But despite her experience of powerlessness and her profound humility, Anastasiia ultimately gained for herself considerable authority: the authority of a *staritsa*, the authority of a mother superior, and the authority of a holy exemplar. This authority of holiness ultimately crossed over traditional class and gender lines: men found themselves seeking the counsel of a woman; and merchant and gentry women, the counsel of a peasant. After her death, the tsar ceded land in her honor, the Nikolaevskii and Kurikha communities continued her memory, and the values of a hierarchical world seemed turned upside down.

One of the sources of confusion in analyzing Anastasiia's life is that she lived in a world of hierarchy and a world outside of hierarchy, a world of the temporal and a world of the infinite. Like many mystics, she lived in both the present and the eternal. As John Caird, the Scottish philosopher of religion, explained:

> Whether we view religion from the human side or the divine—as the surrender of the soul to God, or as the life of God in the soul—in either aspect, it is of its very essence that the infinite has ceased to be a far-off vision, and has become instead a present reality. The very first pulsation of the spiritual life, when we rightly apprehend its significance, is the indication that the division between the spirit and the object has vanished, that the ideal has become real, that the finite has reached its goal and become suffused with the presence and life of the Infinite.[35]

This is also the philosophy, theology, and psychology of the desert ideal—that in living in the life of the spirit, one is living the promised ideal, the eternal present. Anastasiia and the Orthodox tradition often spoke of the life of the spirit as the "angelic life", and often equated it with the monastic life. Before undertaking her life as a hermit, during her near-death experience on the pilgrimage to Murom, Anastasiia had an intense vision in which two youths in white clothes, angelic beings, led her into a church, then past the sacred doors to the holy altar; she then felt herself floating upward, into an angelic choir.[36] This vision is striking, in that it shows Anastasiia's entry into the sacral space of the altar, a place usually forbidden to women in Orthodox churches, as well as her association with angelic beings. The vision can be thought of as a preview of her monastic life, which was based on a gender-free angelic model. As one Orthodox nun has explained: "Since '. . . In Christ there is neither slave nor free, neither male or female . . .' (Gal 3:28), the Orthodox understand gender differences as relating solely to this fallen world. Therefore, the closer one comes to the kingdom of heaven, the less important those differences are. . . . The monastic ideal is to live the 'angelic life' as Adam and Eve did before the Fall."[37] Thus, an analysis of Anastasiia's life and the reactions of people to her, necessarily involves these two perplexing time zones: the present, which is patriarchal and limiting, socially and by gender, and the infinite, where boundaries disappear.

One of the boundaries that disappeared in Anastasiia was the rigid division between the masculine and the feminine. Anastasiia took on many qualities traditionally associated with the masculine. She had a clear sense of self and knew her own path; she followed this path with focus and determination and deep inner listening; she was disciplined and filled with courage (the Russians used the word *muzhestvo* in describing her, which means both courage and manliness); and she exercised considerable authority. In all, she was a tough-spirited woman who was able to integrate her masculine self into a fully human being. The recent writings of feminist theologians have emphasized the importance for women's spirituality of claiming these aspects of self.[38] It can further be argued that holiness, the scripted roles of holy men and women, allows people a fullness, a wholeness beyond our broken, partial roles. Holiness offers men a way of integrating their feminine self through, for example, renunciation and humility, and women a way of integrating their masculine self through acts such as the assertion of inner authority. Perhaps the attractive quality of holiness is in fact wholeness of being, a person who radiates a life force and fresh energy beyond gender. Anastasiia had a freshness of spirit as she discovered and relived the eternal anew. Through prayer and discipline, she connected with her deepest vital life force, the source of spiritual energy; in this lay her strength.

◆ 3 ◆

Service Made Flesh
Matrona Naumovna Popova and the Tikhon-Zadonsk Community

And the idea of pilgrimage renders the journey
important as journey: pilgrimage is significant
journeying. Under its aegis the motion of travel
becomes the action of quest, and so deserving of
reputation.

Mary Campbell,
The Witness and the Other World.

T he life of Matrona Naumovna Popova (1769–185?)
that of Margarita Tuchkova, is primarily a story o
and compassion. But although Margarita's char
form of creating the community that offered poor and
women a better life, Matrona's charity was expressec
spiritual ministry to the strays and wanderers of th
compelling service, particularly to the sick, the
grims, marked her religious vision. Her em
work and an active apostolate anticipated
within Russian women's monastic culture i
from contemplative practice to charitabl

Matrona was born in the town of Elets, in Orlov province, to an impoverished sacristan of the Church of Saints Damian and Cosmos and his overburdened wife. When her father died shortly after she was born, Matrona's family sank into grim poverty. Her older sister was given away to another family, and when Matrona was seven, her mother died, leaving her, an orphan, to care for a paralyzed twelve-year-old brother.[2] Somehow, by running errands, washing laundry, and eating scraps, she managed to keep her brother and herself alive for three years. Her brother then died, leaving her completely alone. At this point, a peasant family, the Abramovs, perhaps spotting a good worker who was no longer burdened with the care of an invalid, took her into their home as a helper both for their children and in the fields. For the next fifteen years, she worked constantly, drawing water, making fires, washing clothes, tending animals, ʰⁱng in the fields.

ˑ and healthy woman, Matrona had many offers of mar-
ᵗᵒ have been drawn inward, toward her own love
ᵎ She found counsel and moral support for
ⁿit, Melaniia, who was renowned for
ⁿ a rocky mountain cliff at the
ⁱsits to her parents, who
ⁿetimes speak with
ᵗrona's great de-
ᵎs Matrona later

unforgettable
versation, in
the limitless
ᵉ lay bare the
ᶠrom the tender
ⁿearthly conver-
ᵉarthly and deceiv-
ᵉ, now lost for once

Deeply moved by this encounter, Matrona wished to take up a life of prayer and to enter the Znamenskii women's monastery, but when she asked Melaniia for her blessing, Melaniia, who had been a disciple of St. Tikhon of Zadonsk (1724–83), urged Matrona instead to go on a pilgrimage to Zadonsk, the area beyond the Don River, to pray before the revered icon of the Vladimir Mother of God and to pay homage at Tikhon's grave. Since it was during the work season, she asked for and received permission from her employers to go on the pilgrimage.[5]

In becoming a pilgrim, Matrona, like Anastasiia Logacheva before her, was following an ancient tradition common to all the world's great religions. Pilgrimage, in the sense of journeys to shrines or holy places for the purpose of veneration, either to obtain favors through the intercession of the holy ones honored there or to give thanks for favors received, is a phenomenon common to all civilizations.[6] The Christian pilgrimage, be it to Jerusalem or Rome or to the sites of local saints and Marian apparitions, always has a purgative and salvific aspect to it. All sites of pilgrimage have this in common:

> They are believed to be places where miracles once happened, still happen, and may happen again. Even where the time of miraculous healings is reluctantly conceded to be past, believers firmly hold that faith is strengthened and salvation better secured by personal exposure to the beneficent unseen presence of the Blessed Virgin or the local saint, mediated through a cherished image or painting.[7]

Miracles and the rekindling of faith are regarded as rewards for undertaking long and frequently perilous journeys, and the journeys themselves have a purgatorial element reminiscent of the Way of the Cross. The pilgrimage offers the pilgrim an opportunity for a forgiveness of sins, a fulfilling of vows, a bodily or spiritual healing, and a new and deeper level of religious experience. In fact, because of the intensity of its effect on the pilgrim, pilgrimage may be considered an exteriorized mysticism, the mystical route of the lay person. As Victor and Edith Turner, anthropologists of religion, have suggested:

> While monastic contemplatives and mystics could daily make interior salvific journeys, those in the world had to exteriorize theirs in the infrequent adventure of pilgrimage. For the majority, pilgrimage was the great liminal experience of the religious life. If mysticism is an interior pilgrimage, pilgrimage is exteriorized mysticism.[8]

Pilgrimage was an important part of the religious landscape of nineteenth-century Russia. Because of a shared religious culture, it was not uncommon for peasants to be given permission by their masters and village communes to go on a pilgrimage, provided it was for a limited time and at a time that did not interfere with the work schedule. Village records indicate that peasants most frequently went on pilgrimage in fulfillment of a vow or for the propitious resolution of an important matter. Young people often went before undertaking marriage; the old, for the forgiveness of sins. The ill often set out in search of healing; the unfortunate, after a calamity such as a fire.[9] Pilgrims sought blessings on new beginnings and help in depression and confusion; they also came to give thanks for favors received.

In addition to those pilgrims (*bogomoltsy*) who had a specific place of pilgrimage as their destination and a journey of limited duration, Russia abounded with holy wanderers (*stranniki*) who made pilgrimage their way of life, journeying from one holy place to the next in search of the sacred. These "mystic vagabonds"[10] viewed pilgrimage as a metaphor for life itself, the path of the earthly sojourner. The Bible describes them thus: "They were not yet in possession of the things promised, but had seen them far ahead and hailed them, and confessed themselves no more than strangers or passing travelers on earth" (Heb 11:13).

Given these cultural factors, the number of pilgrims in nineteenth-century Russia was great, particularly during Holy Week.

Over a million came to Kiev in 1886, the year in which the railroad opened.[11] To a modest monastery such as the Serpukhov Vladych-nyi women's monastery in Moscow province, the number of pilgrims averaged twenty to thirty thousand throughout the 1860s.[12]

Matrona's visit to Zadonsk took place in 1794, eleven years after Tikhon's death. There she felt his abiding presence and heard countless stories of his compassion, his charity, and the unforgettable burning quality of his inner life. Wishing to remain in this place of prayer and deep serenity, she exerted all her strength of will and returned to Elets, to her demanding life with the Abramovs. She found on her return that she could not readjust to the spiritually distracting routine. Something transformative had happened to her at Zadonsk, and she could neither forget the peace she had tasted nor be content with the busy-ness of the world. She soon fell into a state of emotional sickness, a form of "hysteria" in the words of her generally sympathetic biographer, hieromonk Gerontii. She would suddenly drop a tray of dishes she was carrying or fall into a faint. The Abramovs, beginning to suspect that Matrona was acting this way in order to avoid getting married, finally lost patience and dismissed her.[13] Homeless, ill, and without a kopeck to her name, Matrona wandered from place to place, eventually returning to Zadonsk. There, at the grave of St. Tikhon, she was healed of her sickness, a cure that she would forever speak of with deep gratitude and wonder.

After she had recovered, she again wanted to dedicate herself to God and once more asked Melaniia for her blessing on entering the Znamenskii monastery in Elets. It is unclear how Matrona would have afforded entry into the monastery had Melaniia given her blessing. But Melaniia instead told Matrona that she had a special mission to go to Zadonsk, where she should offer shelter to pilgrims and holy wanderers and feed orphans. Matrona later recalled her perplexity at hearing this advice:

It was not without astonishment that I heard the words of my good preceptor, and doubt filled my soul. Not having anything at all of my own, not even acquaintances, in Zadonsk, how could I, I wondered, take in wanderers in Zadonsk, when I myself had no shelter there. . . . But to my inner, secret doubts the penetrating staritsa objected: "Don't doubt, Matrona, but believe."[14]

Further confounding her, Melaniia mysteriously told Matrona that someday she would live in a stone palace and that she would be known not only in but also beyond Moscow.[15] Confused, Matrona resigned herself to divine providence. When she soon after had a dream in which she saw St. Tikhon calling her to Zadonsk, she finally resolved to settle there.

Matrona arrived at Zadonsk frail, dressed in her usual tattered rags, and homeless. At that time (about 1800), the Zadonsk monastery had neither a wayfarers' home nor a hospital to house the increasingly large number of pilgrims who came to venerate this holy site and to seek spiritual and physical healing. Although the exact number of pilgrims coming to Zadonsk during Matrona's lifetime is unknown, the influx steadily increased throughout the first half of the nineteenth century, as the faithful came to venerate St. Tikhon and to view the relics of Mitrofan, former bishop of Voronezh, which were displayed in nearby Voronezh beginning in 1832.[16]

At the time of Matrona's arrival in Zadonsk, Tikhon had not yet been canonized a saint, and the monastery where he reposed, Zadonskii Bogoroditskii men's monastery, had no facilities for pilgrims. Lacking a place to stay and anxious to understand her mission, Matrona prayed by day at the grave of St. Tikhon and slept by night under the open sky. Two monks of the monastery, Anatolii and Ilarii, admiring her faithful vigil, took her under their wing and persuaded a local benefactor to give her a room in his quarters. She soon turned this room into a shelter for other pilgrims. Every day after the church services, she invited back to her room the strays at the monastery, offering them food and a place to sleep. Her reputation for kindness grew, and she began to be known as "Mother-Nurturer" (*matushka-kormilitsa*).[17] The number of people to whom she offered shelter grew so large, and the turnover so great, that the benefactor who had provided her with lodging became distraught and finally asked her to leave. Anatolii and Ilarii then bought her a small hut for twelve rubles near the monastery; there she was able to sleep five or six people at a time, often on a rotating basis, with herself frequently sleeping outdoors. The local authorities became distressed by all this activity and periodically arrested Matrona and some of the wanderers as vagrants. Finally, she was beaten one night in jail and sent back to Elets to get a legal internal passport.[18]

When she returned, she resumed her incorrigible habit of housing and feeding homeless wanderers, again with the help and support of Anatolii and Ilarii, who often brought her food from the monastery or from benefactors. Both monks died soon after this, and she felt deeply bereaved, orphaned once again, as she later told her biographer Gerontii. Gerontii was acutely sensitive to the bereft feelings of an orphan, having himself been orphaned at a young age and placed, at Matrona's advice, in the Zadonsk monastery, where she kept a loving eye on him. In his *Life of Matrona Naumovna Popova*, he refers many times to her special kindness to orphans and the lonely, her particular empathy undoubtedly born of her own painfully forlorn childhood.[19]

Having lost Anatolii and Ilarii, her spiritual friends, she set out on foot on a pilgrimage to Solovetskii monastery, a distance of some nine hundred miles, and then journeyed south to Kiev, the great holy city of Russian Orthodoxy, where she visited the Monastery of the Caves, revered for the wondrously preserved bodies of its ancient saints. Kiev pleased her so much that she wanted to stay there, but twice in a dream, St. Barbara, an early Christian martyr to whom she was particularly devoted, appeared to her telling her of St. Tikhon's great displeasure that she was ignoring her work in Zadonsk. So she set out once again on foot to Zadonsk, to her cabin and her work of feeding and sheltering those in search of the sacred.

After about two years, her mission expanded when a pious merchant offered her the lower floor of his house to be used as a wayfarers' home in honor of his deceased son. At this same time several unmarried women began to gather around Matrona, wishing to emulate her life and her work. They formed the nucleus of the women's religious community of Tikhon-Zadonsk, a community that functioned autonomously for almost forty years, receiving official recognition from church and state authorities only in 1860.[20]

Matrona's life was viewed by her and by her hagiographers as a constant series of prophetic dreams and miraculous coincidences. No sooner did St. Tikhon appear to her in a dream (about fifteen years after the opening of the Wayfarers' Home in the merchant's house), telling her to build a stone shelter for pilgrims and the poor on the northern grounds of the monastery, than a stonemason suddenly appeared offering to do the work on credit. Next, a benefactor unexpectedly gave her two hundred rubles that she was able to use for the building supplies. When the time came for the roof to be put on, an unknown cossack woman suddenly materialized and as suddenly departed, intentionally leaving behind a small bag of gold coins hidden under a pillow. Yet again, when Matrona faced a debt of fifteen hundred rubles for food supplies, a cossack officer wondrously appeared at the door one night, asking agitatedly, "Is it true that you feed pilgrims?" Then he thrust the requisite money into her hands, begged her to pray for him, and abruptly departed.[21] Her faith in God's providence and her disposition to see it at work in the generosity of those who supported her work enabled her to serenely and gratefully pursue a life of charity and compassion without becoming consumed by worry about how she would be able to provide for those in need.

During the cholera epidemic of the early 1830s, her work was especially important. Not only did she endlessly care for the sick, but also her manner of comforting the dying was particularly holy. Acutely sensitive to loneliness, she seems to have sensed the profound aloneness of the human spirit at the moment of death and to have lent this moment grace. She also took great pains to give the dead a decent burial, an ultimate gift of dignity for those without home or family.[22]

In addition to her compassion, other qualities of character marked Matrona as holy in the eyes of her contemporaries. She was skilled in the art of interior prayer, being one "who prayed without ceasing" in the spiritual vocabulary of the time. It was in search of such people that the anonymous pilgrim of the well-known mid-nineteenth-century pilgrim's account, *The Way of the Pilgrim*, wandered throughout the vast spaces of the Russian land, seeking those who could teach him how to fulfill the troubling admonition of St. Paul to "pray without ceasing."[23] Whether sewing garments for the orphans or working with the infirm, Matrona prayed constantly and silently, repeating the rhythmic, centering Jesus prayer so favored by Russian mystics. Thus, although her ministry was more service oriented than that of many contemplatives, for her there was no split between the contemplative and the active life. Constant interior prayer bound both together seamlessly.

Matrona followed a disciplined and regular formal prayer routine. Every day, following morning prayers, she read one *kafizma* (portion of the Psalter) and one *akathist* (hymn of praise to a saint): on Sundays, to Jesus the Savior; on Mondays to her beloved St. Barbara; on Tuesdays, to the revered local saint, Mitrofan of Voronezh; on Thursdays, to St. Nikolai; and on Saturdays, to the Mother of

God. Since Matrona learned to read only late in life, she had memorized certain Psalms as well as the hymns of praise to St. Barbara, the Mother of God, and Christ; other prayers were read aloud by some of the women living in the community that was slowly developing around her.[24] She particularly cherished the ending prayer of the *akathist* to the Mother of God, which included the lines:

> My most gracious Queen, my hope, Mother of God, shelter of orphans, and intercessor of travelers, strangers and pilgrims, joy of those in sorrow, protectress of the wronged, see my distress, see my affliction! Help me for I am helpless. Feed me for I am a stranger and pilgrim. . . . For I know no other help but thee, no other intercessor, no gracious consoler but Thee, O Mother of God, to guard and protect me throughout the ages.[25]

Her long, disciplined years of prayer and good works rendered Matrona wise in the ways of the spirit, and she developed a reputation for great spiritual wisdom and experience. As is archetypically true of a holy sage, her words were listened to carefully and considered sagacious (*prozorlivyi*), and things often came to pass that she had foretold.[26] Both the esteem in which she was held and the humility of her bearing are illustrated by the reminiscence of a visitor to Zadonsk in 1836, who recalls her sitting simply on a wooden bench, quietly praying, while every person who came out of the church, no matter of what rank, bowed to her respectfully as they passed.[27] Another source tells us that not only the inhabitants of the local area but also eminent secular and clerical figures sought spiritual guidance from her; Antonii, the bishop of Voronezh, held her up as a model of the apostolic life.[28] Matrona had achieved the authority of holiness, that moral respect given to the righteous despite their own view of themselves as the most unworthy of creatures.

Matrona, both in words and bearing, spoke a language of humility while living a life of actual spiritual authority. This simultaneous indwelling of humility and authority was also present in the hermit Anastasiia. For Matrona, holiness included the acquisition of authority and largesse. The founder of the Wayfarers' Home and the distributor of alms, shelter, and hospitality, Matrona, a woman born to poverty, unconsciously played out the magnanimous virtues of the wealthy. One of her dreams sharply illustrates this. In the dream, St. Tikhon instructed her to build a stone shelter for wanderers on the northern part of the monastery grounds, greeting her with the words "It is time, Matrona, for you yourself to become a proprietress" (*khoziaika*, owner or mistress of a home).[29] This dream recurred three times, and it is not difficult for us to sense the emotional power for Matrona, who had been orphaned, homeless, and for many years a domestic servant at the beck and call of her mistress, of these role-reversing words that portrayed her as the mistress and proprietress of her own home and a generous provider to others. And Melaniia's prophecy that Matrona would live in a stone palace (the Wayfarers' Home was built of stone) and be known in Moscow and beyond also relied for its wonder on the class reversals in which a low-born woman might become famous and rich. Because one of the marks of Christian holiness is the radical transformation of human nature that follows a turning to the divine, holiness is often revealed in the turning of worldly values upside down, as, for example, a rich aristocratic woman like Margarita Tuchkova taking on the life-style of the poor, or a humble peasant like Anastasiia Logacheva or Matrona Popova acquiring spiritual authority and a beneficent largess.

Available sources reveal that Matrona's relationship to her community differed from that of Margarita. Whereas Margarita was strongly attached to the sisters of her community, Matrona lavishes her love on orphans and wayfarers, the strays and the dying. Although pious women gathered around her as helpers and disciples, she did not make plans to formally establish a community until shortly before her death. During all these years, she and her women coworkers (*sotrudnitsy*) had been living in the Wayfarers' Home she had founded on the grounds of the Zadonskii Bogoroditskii men's monastery, feeding, sheltering, and nursing sick and distressed pilgrims. Although they attended liturgy in the monastery church, they performed some of their prayer disciplines, including the reading of the Psalter for the dead, in Matrona's cell.[30] In her last years, Matrona seemed to have strongly desired to acquire formal recognition by the Synod of this community of women as well as their own buildings and chapel. She gave the Wayfarers' Home she had built to the Zadonsk monastery and settled with her coworkers on property on the edge of town, which had been donated by benefactors. In her will, which she gave to her spiritual confessor, she asked him to help her in the "building of a community for her coworkers on the place left by her, at which there should be a small church in the name of the Most Sorrowful Mother of God."[31] In June of 1851, three months before her death, Matrona gave a letter to a nun who was setting out on a pilgrimage to Moscow, addressed to Antonii, archimandrite of the Holy Trinity St. Sergius Monastery, requesting help from him and Metropolitan Filaret in obtaining recognition for her community. Antonii passed the letter on to Filaret, who submitted a petition to the Synod on December 2, 1851, accompanied by a letter to the over-procurer of the Synod, Count N. A. Protasov. Filaret's letter is a skillful combination of piety and calculation, extolling the virtues of the Tikhon Zadonsk community, while assuring the Synod that there would be no financial burden in giving the community official status. Recognizing that as metropolitan of the diocese of Moscow he had no business interfering in the affairs of the diocese of Voronezh where Zadonsk was located, Filaret's letter begins:

> It is necessary to acknowledge that I am entering into another's business, in presenting to Your Eminence a petition of the Tikhonovskoe

Society of sisters of mercy, which has existed in Zadonsk for about forty
years, without this name, and without legal establishment, but which
now, according to the Last Will and Testament of the founder, Matrena
Naumova (*sic*), is seeking legal recognition.·

I know that matters of philanthropy receive the attention and care
of Your Eminence even without petition. Nevertheless, Naumova, I
don't know why, having wanted to use me for petitioning on this matter, I decided not to refuse, partly because I have heard of her God-
pleasing works, and partly because she, after expressing her
above-mentioned wish, has died; and it is not as easy to contradict
and refuse those who have gone to God, as those living on earth.

Filaret then went on to praise the community for its charitable activity and its Russian spirit, saying:

If it is worthy to establish women's communities which have as
their goal only the personally quiet and pious life of the sisters, then
it is possible to propose that it is no less, or indeed even more, worthy to establish a community which joins to the aforementioned
goal, the rendering of brotherly love to our poorest neighbors. And it
is good that the Tikhonovskoe community has formed itself not according to a foreign model, but in the simplicity of spirit of the Orthodox and Russian.

Finally, he assured Protasov that the community would not be a financial burden to the state, arguing that although the community
did not have strong financial resources, if it acted in the true spirit of
faith and trust in God, it could count on Russian philanthropy to
support it. And if, God forbid, it should become impoverished, then
"the members of the society, as those not tied by permanent vows,
can return to the rank to which they belong, and the life of the community will be extinguished as quietly as it quietly began."[32]

It is doubtful that Matrona drew up the elaborate charter for the
community, which was officially recognized by the Synod in 1860,
though it did faithfully reflect the type of charitable work to which
she had devoted her life. Her own words of instruction to her

followers were quite simple. Drawing them to her on her deathbed, she entrusted them to the Queen of Heaven and the mercy of God. She then chose the most experienced of them as mother superior and tearfully prevailed on them to carry out, with all their fervor, their work and service on behalf of the suffering.[33] The archbishop of Voronezh, under whose protection the community would eventually fall, also advised them simply: "Work, children, for the good of your neighbor. God will not abandon you. Imitate in all things your good eldress [Matrona] and honor her."[34]

In imitation of the life of Matrona, the officially established community of St. Tikhon of Zadonsk had an active apostolate dedicated to nursing and caring for wandering pilgrims, and its work centered around the new Wayfarers' Home at the edge of town. According to its charter, which was drawn up at the behest of the Synod, the sisters of the Wayfarers' Home were to be accepted by the mother superior from among women of all social estates, who wished "for the glory of God to serve suffering humanity in the person of wandering pilgrims who have come to the town of Zadonsk for veneration of the holy relics of St. Tikhon and who visit the Wayfarers' Home for soothing from the toils of the road, or for healing of spiritual and bodily ailments."

The women accepted into the community should be of "irreproachable character, ready for every kind of service, and disposed to a God-pleasing life." They had to be at least twenty years old and to have legal documentation. They were to wear simple clothes of black cloth, preferably in the same style. They were, above all, obligated to "unselfishly and fervently" serve the wanderers and pilgrims who were being sheltered in the Wayfarers' Home, taking especial care of "the sick and meek." The religious duties of the sisters included observing the four great fasts[35] and confessing and receiving Holy Communion. In addition, all of them were to know by heart the Apostles' Creed and the Lord's Prayer and other short prayers used before and after meals in the refectory, as well as short prayers for vespers and matins. All work was to begin with a prayer and be performed in a spirit of quiet and serenity, accompanied, when appropriate, by the reading of passages from Scripture or the Lives of the Saints by a literate sister.[36]

The pilgrims visiting the Wayfarers' Home were to be accepted for three days at all times of the year if they had passports and were in sober condition. There were to be separate quarters for them, and they would be provided with simple food consisting of bread, *kvass* (a peasant drink made from bread), one hot dish, and kasha. Weak and sick pilgrims were to be housed in special rooms, where they would be taken care of by sisters especially assigned to this duty by the mother superior by virtue of their "ability and vocation." The sisters were obliged to provide "the most zealous care" of these needy, giving them necessary medicine as ordered by a doctor and providing a special diet for them. The poor and needy who recovered from their illness would be given money for their journey at the time of their departure, whereas those who died would be properly buried and their souls prayed for in the chapel of the Wayfarers' Home.[37]

Although the charter and purpose of the community are quite explicit, there is some confusion about the exact title of the community formed in Zadonsk. Although the charter refers in its heading to the "Tikhon women's community with a Wayfarers' Home," Filaret referred to it as the "Tikhonovskoe Society of sisters of mercy" in his letter to the over-procurer of the Synod in 1851.[38] The use of the term *sisters of mercy* is of particular interest, since it is believed that the sisters of mercy evolved in Russia during the Crimean War (1853–56) partly in imitation of Florence Nightingale's nurses and the French Catholic sisters of mercy.[39] In fact, the first Russian community of sisters of mercy was founded in 1844 on the initiative of

Grand Duchess Aleksandra Nikolaevna and Princess Tereziia Ol'denburgskaia and in a spirit reminiscent of those of European Catholic orders, with broad goals such as the care of the sick, abandoned children, and fallen women.[40] Filaret might have favored the term *sisters of mercy* in referring to Matrona's community to emphasize its nursing and charitable work and to make the point that such charitable work could grow naturally from the Orthodox tradition rather than relying on foreign, non-Orthodox models. He stressed to the Synod that such a community had formed, not according to a foreign model, but "in the simplicity of spirit of the Orthodox and Russian."Filaret was responding to the increasing criticism, beginning in the middle of the nineteenth century, of Orthodox monasticism for an excessive emphasis on contemplation and ritual to the exclusion of good works.[41] Because Russia, unlike the West, had experienced not a religious reformation or counterreformation, there had been no Protestant debunking of monasticism, celibacy, and the contemplative life, and no formation of specialized women's religious orders dedicated to an active apostolate, which had marked the Reformation in Europe. Within the nineteenth-century Russian context, Matrona was a trailblazer in her emphasis on structured charitable work as part of a dedicated religious life. She and her coworkers took literally the simple maxims of the Bible to love one's neighbor as one's self: to feed the hungry, clothe the naked, shelter the homeless, visit the sick, and bury the dead.

In the second half of the nineteenth century, a distinction developed between societies of sisters of mercy (*obshchestva sester miloserdia*) and women's religious communities (*zhenskie obshchiny*). Although both had their roots in a religious impulse, the societies of sisters of mercy took on a more secular character, with lay women filling their ranks and eventually forming the core of a nursing profession.[42] (The religious roots of the nursing profession are still revealed in the former Soviet Union, where the Russian word for nurse is sister). *Zhenskie obshchiny* became clearly associated with monastic communities and, by the late nineteenth century, were viewed as the formative stage of a women's monastery, preparatory to its official elevation to that higher status. The sisters of the community were increasingly considered novices, with monastic profession assumed to be their goal. But these women's religious communities, and the monasteries that emerged from them, undertook more charitable work than the traditional Orthodox monastic model, with its emphasis on the contemplative life, envisioned. Over thirty-six women's religious communities began as almshouses, and in the second half of the nineteenth century, women's religious communities frequently ran orphanages and schools as well as ministering to elderly and homeless women.[43] Matrona's community was among these groups.

On the eve of World War I, there were fifty-one nuns and 128 novices who, in the spirit of Matrona, combined religious discipline with charitable activity. Together they ran, in addition to the Wayfarers' Home, a parish school for seventy girls and a handicraft school for a dozen girls. They continued to shelter and nurse the pilgrims who came to Zadonsk, including those who came especially on August 17, the anniversary of Matrona's death, for a commemorative liturgy.[44] It is fitting that the burial place of Matrona, who in her own lifetime had shown such reverence for the grave of St. Tikhon, should itself become a place of pilgrimage and homage.[45] In commemorating Matrona, these faithful were commemorating a spirit of compassion, a life lived in love and service to the poor, the lonely, and the sick. Matrona was not a religious abstraction but a real woman who gave up her own cot to let others sleep under a roof, who shared her coarse food with those whose stomachs were growling, who gently changed the soiled bandages and bedclothes of the sick and hurt, and who comforted the dying and nurtured the young and the orphaned.

In her works of charity, particularly with the young, the sick, and the old, she exemplified virtues that nineteenth-century women added to the Russian monastic model. A comparison of the charitable activities of men's and women's monasteries in the early twentieth century clearly indicates a greater preponderance of charitable activities in the women's monasteries.[46] In addition, men's monastic charity differed from women's: men's monasteries were more inclined toward education, particularly of older boys, whereas women's monasteries more often took care of people at their most vulnerable stages—as orphans, as young children, as homeless, as elderly, as the dying. Matrona was a prototype of this development, a representative of the countless number of women who, through the communities they founded and joined, put their stamp on the Russian monastic model, making it more compassionate, communal, and service oriented. If women like Anastasiia could integrate a masculine self through her courageous asceticism, so could women like Matrona add a feminine, compassionate spirit to the contemplative life. Embodying the ideal of service, Matrona embodied a key aspect of women's religious vision.

◆4◆

The Urgency of Salvation

Mother Angelina and the Women of the Tvorozhkovo Community

In these monasteries each nun had the opportunity
to develop her own talent, whether in the household, in field work, in marketing or selling, in administration, in a handicraft or a skilled craft.
Claire Claus, "Die Russischen Frauenklöster."

aised in the luxury of a St. Petersburg townhouse and married at an early age, Mother Angelina (1809–80) spent the first half of her life enmeshed in marital responsibilities while aching for a more contemplative life. Her story, like that of Anastasiia and Matrona, is a story of waiting on God. It is also a testimony to her belief in the radical importance of salvation and her determination to create a community that would offer women of all classes, rich and poor, an enhanced chance of redemption through the monastic life.

Christened Aleksandra Filippovna Shmakova, she was born in 1809 to wealthy noble parents, who were known for their piety and good works.[1] Her father loved to go to church, always choosing to stand and pray among the poor rather than with the well-to-do, believing the prayers of the humble to be a more potent vehicle to God's mercy. He often went on pilgrimages to local holy places and visited the Monastery of the Caves in Kiev several times. Her mother was quite strict with her, teaching her lessons from the Bible and fundamental Christian precepts, but her grandmother doted on her. At the age of seven, despite her grandmother's protests, she was packed off to the elite Smol'nyi Institute for Noble Girls in St. Petersburg, founded by Empress Catherine the Great in 1764. The curriculum included Scripture and the catechism as well as good manners and morals, foreign languages, dancing, and music.[2] She studied there for seven years, graduating with high distinction in 1823. The following year, just after turning fifteen, she was married to a wealthy Baltic Russian nobleman, Karl Andreevich Fon-Roze, a Lutheran. Despite the mutual affection that developed between Aleksandra and her husband, an opulent new home, and a wide circle of friends, Aleksandra felt a gnawing discontent. Her soul always seemed sad, and she was bored by the vanities of the world. She dreamed of building her own chapel, where she could escape from the bustle and vacuousness of the St. Petersburg social scene. One day this dream crystallized into a sudden impulse to build a large church and dedicate it to the Holy Trinity, that profoundly mysterious representation of God as Father, Son, and Holy Spirit. As she later explained to a friend: "It happened that I, a sinner, surrounded with luxury and wealth, was out riding one day decked out in a fashionable riding outfit on an fine trotter, and the whole time a thought kept intensifying in me: Oh! if God would send me the happiness of building a church! It will without fail be built in the name of the Holy Trinity! And how happy I will be then."[3] Aleksandra had no idea of how she would bring this to pass, and it was in fact only after thirty years and many sorrows that she was able to fulfill this burning wish.

In the end of 1847, after twenty-three years of marriage, a daughter was born to Aleksandra and her husband, to their great joy. Mariia was a delightfully sweet and gentle baby, God's little angel, as her mother called her. But that same God seemed to call Mariia back to him. In early January of 1849, at a little more than a year old, Mariia died.

Aleksandra and her husband sank into deep despair. How were they to understand the painful mystery of a gift given and a gift as quickly taken away? Aleksandra was alternately brokenhearted, angry, and inconsolable. Her grief seared her deeply, but with time she found consolation through her faith in God's ultimate purpose and goodness. As she later told a close friend:

> Our Gracious Father sent me sorrow—he took away my daughter, who was such a comfort to me. During that difficult time, I thought that no one on earth had such a sorrow as I did; I grieved, I cried, I grumbled at God, but He the Most Merciful was concerned only with my salvation. From that time I awakened as from a dream. All the luxury, vanity, and glitter of this temporal life became a great burden to me. I began to understand that the only comfort is in God. To love the poor and to go to church became an urgent need for me. How happy I felt on that day, when God helped me share with the poor all the blessings which I had received from him.[4]

She began to visit the poor and the imprisoned in the wretched, stinking slums and the frightening dungeons of tsarist Petersburg.[5] As salvation became more acutely important to her, she began to worry about the salvation of her Lutheran husband. She prayed day and night for his conversion to Orthodoxy, but to no avail. Her way of life became increasingly ascetic. She lived for many days off of one serving of porridge, which evoked derision among her servants, who sometimes called her food "dog food." Her severe way of life eventually led to strain with her husband, who occasionally criticized her abusively.

Feeling constricted in her spiritual life and sadly at odds with her husband, she thought of leaving him and entering a convent. She sought out spiritual counselors, holy men and women who could help her carry out her plan. But she found that none of them counseled her to leave her husband and enter a monastery. To a person, they believed it wrong for her to leave her husband, since she might be the cause of sin both for him and for herself. Instead, they urged her to live in peace with him. She should pray earnestly and have faith that God eventually would arrange things for her salvation.

Aleksandra did not like this advice but nonetheless submitted to it. She continued her good works of visiting the poor and imprisoned and lived simply, trusting in God's will. With time, her simplicity and inner peace touched her husband, and he began to think there must be something powerful in Orthodoxy. To Aleksandra's great joy, he converted to Orthodoxy, taking the name Nikolai, one of the most beloved of Russian saints.[6]

Thus began a period of great happiness and spiritual closeness for Aleksandra and Nikolai. Together they prayed, together they worked and distributed goods to the poor. Since neither had any close or needy relatives, Nikolai began to think about what they could best do with their property. After much reflection, he earnestly proposed to Aleksandra that after their death, they build a monastery, saying, "If it should happen that you die before me, I will build a men's monastery, but if I die before you, you can build a women's cloister; that way we will always be able to help each other through prayers and we won't experience separation."[7] Aleksandra took this to heart and suggested they begin looking for a suitable place to build a monastery. In the beginning of 1858, with the help of Nikolai's brother-in-law, Mr. Gol'derman (the husband of Nikolai's deceased sister), Nikolai purchased the estate of Tvorozhkovo in Gdovskii district west of St. Petersburg, where Gol'derman also had property.

Aleksandra was appalled when she first saw the property, a desolate, monotonous piece of land with dilapidated barns and sheds and a decrepit cottage. But Nikolai reassured her, saying that with its woods, nearby lake, and distance from other settlements, the property would make a wonderful place for a monastery. So they decided in the spring of 1858 to live on the property and begin to work the land. They settled into the cottage, which was divided in two by an old crumbling wall. On one side, there was a relatively large room and a kitchen, where Aleksandra and Nikolai lived together with one servant, their trusted housekeeper; on the other side lived a few serfs, their work hands. Nikolai himself began to fell the trees for the timber needed for a new, larger house. In the process, he caught a bad cold, which developed into a serious illness, and he died in June. His last wishes were that Aleksandra should free their serfs, build a church, and begin the work of establishing a women's monastic community at Tvorozhkovo.[8]

Aleksandra was forty-nine years old and devastated. She had lost her husband of thirty-four years just when they had become soul mates, loving spiritual companions to each other. But in time, she sensed that this was also an opportunity for her to actualize some of her long-held dreams: to build a church in honor of the Holy Trinity, to enter a convent, and to free herself from the moral burdens of property ownership. She was therefore very distressed when Gol'derman proposed marriage to her. She made it clear to him that although she valued his friendship and was grateful to him for his help in her time of distress and confusion, she was not interested in marrying again. After a brief, awkward period, their friendship resumed. Shortly after this, however, he became seriously ill. Aleksandra visited him frequently at his estate, which was only about two miles from Tvorozhkovo. Fearing for his eternal salvation, she strenuously urged on each visit that he convert to Orthodoxy; he as vigorously refused. A few days before his death, he struck a difficult bargain with Aleksandra: he told her that he would agree to receive the Orthodox ritual of the anointing of the sick if she would agree to marry him if he got better.

This bargain tested Aleksandra to the core. In her view, the salvation of a soul was at stake. Her own desires seemed secondary in comparison with this awesome fact. After much soul searching, she agreed. The priest was sent for, Gol'derman was anointed, and died shortly after.[9]

Now Aleksandra felt completely alone, without relatives or close friends. She spent the winter in St. Petersburg but could not find any like-minded spirits among her acquaintances. In the summer she returned to Tvorozhkovo, taking up agricultural work as well as the management of the estate. She also visited many convents, familiarizing herself with monastic life and mulling over how to realize her and her husband's dream of turning Tvorozhkovo into a religious community. Believing as she did in the supreme importance of eternal salvation over the temporal nature of life on earth and convinced that monastic life offered the surest path to salvation, she wanted to offer poor women the same opportunity available to more well-to-do women to lead this dedicated existence. She also dreamed of someday opening a school or an orphanage for the local children, since opportunities for education and religious instruction were sadly lacking in a backwoods region like Tvorozhkovo.[10]

But Aleksandra lacked the means for such ambitious plans. Unlike Margarita Tuchkova, she had no powerful protectors with good connections, and her finances were inadequate to the goal. Her husband, according to her biographer Snessoreva, had, out of the generosity of his heart, lent sixty thousand rubles of her capital to various people, and she was able to call back only eleven thousand rubles from these loans.[11] She would need all of this and more for the construction of a large dwelling and a church at Tvorozhkovo. She decided to rent her home in St. Petersburg for a good income and simultaneously began plans for the freeing of her serfs.

In 1859 Aleksandra submitted a petition to Metropolitan Grigorii for permission to build a women's religious community at Tvorozhkovo. After much delay, he refused on the grounds that there was already a parish church nearby. He suggested instead that she build a community near the village of Zvanka on the empty Derzhavin estate. This displeased Aleksandra. She did not like her local parish church and, after visiting Zvanka, knew that she did not like that locale. She grumbled at the thought of spending all of her money to build a community in a place that had no meaning for her and where she would be unable to fulfill her husband's wishes that a religious community be established at Tvorozhkovo, the place they had shared. She finally wrote a letter to the metropolitan declining to build a community at Zvanka. She continued to plan for a community at Tvorozhkovo. Her faith and her determination saw her through several difficult, discouraging years. Trusting that Tvorozhkovo would one day become a religious community, she continued to live and work there. After her serfs were offered freedom, only three decided to stay with her: her trusted housekeeper and two male serfs, one deaf and the other dimwitted. They lived together in the run-down cottage, which was cold and damp. In the winter, the snow blew into one corner, and whoever slept there got covered with a wet blanket of snow. Aleksandra's housekeeper describes this period vividly:

> We would be covered by snow. The Mistress would come to us and blow the snow off of us, and we would do the same to her. We suffered much grief. . . . It was very hard for me, almost more than was fair for one person. It happened one time that I was so tired from work, that I began to cry. And all the other peasants taunted me: why

are you staying, you fool? nothing's ever going to be there; there isn't going to be a holy cloister! I dearly loved the good mistress, but lost patience and became fainthearted.

When Aleksandra had to go to St. Petersburg one time on business, her faithful housekeeper (who remains nameless in the sources) became despondent, crying day and night on account of the isolation and the work. On the verge of leaving, she had a dream in which a woman appeared to her, asking her why she was crying and assuring her comfortingly that a monastic community would be built there; many would gather, seeking salvation. When Aleksandra returned, the housekeeper told her about the dream. Aleksandra thought it was a wonderful blessing, telling her joyously that the Mother of God herself had come and consoled her.[12]

Like her housekeeper, Aleksandra was taunted by her acquaintances, who asked her why she was foolish enough to give up the luxury of her St. Petersburg home for such a difficult life at Tvorozhkovo. But she took literally the words of the Bible, that earthly riches are worthless, that one must above all seek the Kingdom of God. When she was asked why she thought she had to enter a monastery when it was perfectly possible to save one's soul in the world, she replied "I am so weak and fainthearted that it is hard for me to seek salvation in the midst of worldly bustle."[13]

During this time she found support for her plans from Bishop Agafangel, who prayed with her and encouraged her to persevere. He gave her what he said should be the first building block for the community, an icon of the Mother of God from Mt. Athos. The icon had a revered place in the community until the revolution of 1917.

When Metropolitan Grigorii died in 1861, she immediately petitioned his successor, Isidor, for permission to build a women's religious community. He promised to help her and in August 1862 began the process of applying for official approval from the Holy

Synod. Using the timber Nikolai had cut four years before, Aleksandra immediately began the construction of a large wooden building that would contain a chapel and living quarters for the women she hoped would gather. She prayed earnestly that God would send her hard-working, spiritual women who would be willing to struggle together in the creation of a holy refuge. One by one, they came, seeking a pious life and willing to work long and zealously like their model, Aleksandra. In June of 1865 they received the good news that their growing community, which numbered fifteen at the time, had been officially recognized by the Holy Synod and given the name Holy Trinity Tvorozhkovo women's community (Sviato-Troitskaia Tvorozhkovskaia zhenskaia obshchina).[14]

By 1865 the designation by the Synod of a community of women as a *zhenskaia obshchina* meant that the community was coming under the protection and supervision of the church hierarchy. It also meant that the community was seen as a proto-monastic institution, a transitional, trial stage before elevation to the higher, official stage of a "monastery." The latter involved the appointment of regular clergy and the opportunity for those sisters who wished to become professed nuns to take permanent vows, as opposed to the temporary vows of women in a women's religious community.

Aleksandra was appointed mother superior of the newly recognized Holy Trinity Tvorozhkovo women's community. She eagerly began preparations for the dedication of the chapel and the beginning of a real monastic routine. The sisters worked hard decorating the chapel and sewing and embroidering liturgical vestments, altar cloths, and their own monastic habits. An experienced nun from the Zverin convent in Novgorod came for six months to help establish a monastic routine. She taught the sisters how to read Church Slavonic (the language of the liturgy) and instructed them in the correct behavior and attitude for church, the refectory, and their communal and individual assignments. The sisters recounted long afterward the providential way God sent them four women with beautiful voices to form the core of a choir. As the time for the dedication of the chapel drew near, Aleksandra had become distraught, realizing that there were no women with good voices to sing the beautiful Orthodox liturgy. She prayed to God to send them singers for the choir. At just this time, a local young peasant woman named Marfa, who was familiar with the struggling new community at Tvorozhkovo, developed a sudden urge to go on a pilgrimage to Cheremenetskii monastery. While there, she happened to overhear melodic singing coming from the direction of four young peasant women. The women were on their way to the diocese of Novgorod to enter the Korotskia women's community, but Marfa, extolling the praises of Aleksandra, persuaded them instead to join the Tvorozhkovo community. They were particularly impressed that Aleksandra, a *barynia*, had given all her property to the community and "herself worked alongside of the sisters." They came to Tvorozhkovo and, after receiving instruction in liturgical singing from a music theorist specially hired by Aleksandra, developed into a beautiful choir, the pride of the area.[15]

Finally, on a cold day in December 1866, the chapel, ablaze with candles, was dedicated. Aleksandra was tonsured as a ryassaphore nun (postulant) and took the monastic name Angelina. Abbot Antonii, who was celebrating the liturgy, remarked on the appropriateness of the name, for in entering the monastic order, she was entering the angelic order. The sisters, adorned in their new black habits, were all there, some beaming, some moved to tears. Aleksandra, now Mother Angelina, had herself dressed each one of them that morning, noting as she put on their black garb that in choosing the monastic life they were dying to the world. Their black habit, as she explained, was symbolically a coffin for those wishing to become nuns.[16]

The number of women wishing to "flee the world" and take up a dedicated religious life at Tvorozhkovo continued to grow. By 1872 the number of sisters had grown to twenty-six and included two widows of government officials, a woman from the merchant class, one from the clerical estate, eight from the artisan class, and thirteen from the peasant class.[17] In 1877 there were thirty-one sisters and Mother Angelina. Archival records indicate that twenty-six of the women were peasants.[18]

Mother Angelina's dream of offering poor women a means of living a monastic life supportive of their salvation was becoming a reality. Unlike the traditional monasteries, which expected substantial monetary donations for entry and were often located in cities and provincial towns, a communally organized agricultural community like Tvorozhkovo offered women without means the chance to contribute to the support of the community through their labor and handicrafts.[19]

Like its prototype, the early Christian community, the communal monastic life was, in Angelina's view, a great equalizer: one's worldly station was forgotten and everyone worked, prayed, and shared together in peace and love. Simple monastic dress helped obliterate class distinctions. As Mother Angelina reminded the sisters, those who put on monastic dress and willingly undertook a new spiritual life had to bear bodily and spiritual labor without complaint and carry their cross to the end with self-renunciation. She urged the new community:

> Let us all forget our rank in the world and let us all work in love for God. Live among each other peacefully and I will rejoice with you. The Merciful Lord gives us heavenly bread and also cares about us on earth. Don't abandon hope in Him, and He will never abandon us, if only we lead our lives in constant work and prayer, and without murmuring.[20]

Constant work and prayer aptly characterize the lives of Angelina and the women of the Tvorozhkovo community. Angelina's estate, which she had donated for the support of the community, consisted of over sixteen hundred acres. The sisters worked it all themselves: they reaped the harvest and threshed it, plowed the land, mowed the hay, chopped wood. At night they took turns acting as guard, since the grounds of the community were still not enclosed by a wall. Angelina supervised the work and herself shared in the heavy labor. She also took part in the housecleaning and washed her own laundry, considering it a sin to make someone else clean up her dirty things. Her old housekeeper often clucked to herself, remembering the pampered life to which Angelina had been accustomed.[21] But Angelina felt very much at home, having finally found a community of like-minded women.

In addition to agricultural work and handicrafts, Angelina and the sisters of the community ran an almshouse (in modern terms, a nursing home) for six elderly poor women. When they had completed the construction of a two-story building to serve as an orphanage, Angelina turned her considerable energies to the fulfillment of a lifelong dream—building a stone church in honor of the Holy Trinity.

The building of the church required substantial financial resources and ecclesiastical approval. Angelina had set aside seven thousand rubles of the money that was originally hers for this purpose; in addition, there were about three thousand rubles saved from income that could be used for building materials. Even though this amount was inadequate for such an ambitious project, Angelina wrote to the St. Petersburg consistory in 1873, requesting permission to build a stone church and arguing that this was the ardent wish of the sisters, since they had long outgrown their tiny chapel. While waiting for approval, she began plans for the construction of the church and the purchase of some building materials, and was later reprimanded for her impatience. Despite the rebuke, she eventually received authorization for the church. In 1875 the St. Petersburg consistory appointed a building committee to supervise the construction, with Angelina being the most energetic member.[22] From then until her death in 1880, she worked round the clock, soliciting donations of money, labor, and supplies and supervising every detail of the creation of what she prayed would be a splendid and lasting tribute to the Holy Trinity. The church was completed in 1882; in 1887 the community was elevated to a monastery.[23] The sisters were, as Angelina had wished, predominantly from the poorer classes. According to the records of the St. Petersburg consistory, in 1897 Trinity Tvorozhkovo monastery had grown to fifty-nine: of the thirteen nuns, ten were peasants and three from the lower bureaucracy; the one novice was from the artisan class, and the forty-five sisters included thirty-six peasants.[24] In 1907 the monastery had grown again, to seventy-nine, with an abbess, seventeen nuns, ten novices, and fifty-one sisters; of these, sixteen of the nuns, all ten of the novices, and forty-five of the fifty-one sisters were peasants.[25]

The economic resources of the community were typical of Russian women's religious communities, combining income from agricultural work, the religious services of the sisters, and donations from benefactors. According to an 1888 report, the yearly income of the community included two thousand rubles from land, one thousand rubles from the rental of the St. Petersburg home of a benefactress, interest from the ten thousand rubles in fixed capital donated by Mother Angelina and from three thousand rubles donated by benefactors, one thousand rubles from collections on behalf of the community, three hundred rubles from the perpetual reading of the Psalter for the deceased, one thousand rubles from the cattle yard, and one thousand rubles from church and candle income.[26]

The monastery's sixteen hundred acres of land included plow land, hay land, forest land, and three lakes. Rye, oats, hay, flax, and all garden vegetables were grown on the land and were sufficient, in good harvest, for the needs of the monastery for the whole year; in bad harvest, grain had to be purchased. When Snessoreva, Mother Angelina's biographer, wrote her history of the community in 1887 on the occasion of its elevation to a monastery, she visited the monastery and was inspired by the communal work of the sisters and the effect on the neighboring peasants:

> The people see how from year to year from the first days of spring, the sisters, under the direction of their mother superior, rush to work, clear the fields. . . . (At harvest) they gather in the mown hay and bring it to the barn, and for this all the elderly women from the almshouse and all the orphans from the orphanage gather; then these same sisters begin the harvesting of grain, they themselves reap and grind it, and then in the evenings, contented but extremely tired, they return home, singing Psalms—the people, seeing this, are touched by the spirit, and involuntarily cross themselves and utter with all their heart, "May God help you, holy workers."[27]

Between communal work such as harvesting and their individual assigned duties, or "obediences" (*poslushaniia*), the women of the community were offered considerable opportunity to exercise responsibility and initiative. Someone had to be in charge of the orphanage, the almshouse, the library, the garden, the cattle yard, the bakery, the dairy, the choir, the treasury. A detailed analysis of the monastery's annual reports to the St. Petersburg consistory, which include the duties assigned to each sister, reveals the wide range of responsibilities taken on by the women of the community, including peasant women. In 1877, for example, the treasurer of the community, the second-in-command to Mother Angelina, was a forty-eight-year-old woman from the merchant class; in 1897 the nun Estolia, a peasant, was serving as treasurer.[28] Peasant women served as stewards, directors of the choir, and managers of the dairy, the cattle yard, the orphanage, and the monastery's inn as well as being in charge of agricultural husbandry and the preservation of vegetables. They had considerable opportunity to develop and exercise their abilities and had significantly higher literacy rates than the average peasant woman.[29]

Prayer was central to the life of the community. Although a sufficient supply of priests was difficult to find in the vast spaces of rural Russia, Angelina arranged through the clergy of the local parish church and the Cheremenetskii monastery to have services at least four times a week. In addition, the sisters chanted the Psalter regularly.

Angelina's own prayer routine was very strict. At the end of a hard day of work and administrative responsibility, she would drag herself into her cell to begin her long, nightly prayer discipline, which unfailingly included the reading of the *akathist* to the Savior (which is twenty-four pages long) and the reading of the *akathist* to the Mother of God (which is twenty-five pages long).[30] When her cell servant (a novice assigned to older nuns for apprenticeship) observed her to be particularly exhausted, she would suggest that perhaps tonight she could shorten her prayers. Angelina would answer, "No, my dear, I can't lie down without saying my prayers. What will happen if I lie down, and don't get up till doomsday? Putting aside prayers can't be done. As the body demands food, so a soul can't live without prayers."[31] When she had finished her prayers, she would stand in her cell and bless each one of the sisters, most of whom were long since asleep, by making the sign of the cross in the direction of each one's cell. Then she blessed all of the animals belonging to the community. In the summer, she always asked where the horses were pastured for the night so she could turn in that direction when sending them her blessing. Given her love of this pastoral life, one can imagine how passionately she would have intoned to the Mother of God the section of the *akathist* praising her miraculous fertility:

> Rejoice, branch of an Unfading Sprout!
> Rejoice, acquisition of Immortal Fruit!
> Rejoice, laborer that laborest for the Lover of mankind!
> Rejoice, thou who givest birth to the Planter of our
>   life!
> Rejoice, cornland yielding a rich crop of mercies![32]

During her lifetime, Angelina was overpowered with the urgency of salvation, both for herself and for others. She distributed the money she received from her husband's pension among the poor, asking them to pray for his soul. She arranged that every Sunday after the liturgy, a memorial service (*panakhida*) be offered for the dead. She herself reverently intoned the long list of the departed for whom the prayers were offered.[33] On her deathbed she requested that the sisters continue this practice, asked their forgiveness for any wrongs she had done them, and begged them to remember her in their prayers.[34]

Angelina had faithfully waited on God while resolutely planning a religious community for women. She saw in every human being a soul thirsting, like hers, for eternal life. Impelled by the Orthodox belief in the monastic life as a more perfect means of salvation, her compassion and charity took the form of offering all women, regardless of class, the opportunity to seek their own salvation. There was, she believed, no more urgent equality than this.

◆ 5 ◆

Inner Visions and Outer Struggles

Abbess Taisiia and the Angelic Life

"Feminist ideology" is another word for trying to
understand, in the life of a woman, the life of the
mind, which is, as Nancy Miller has noted, "not
coldly cerebral, but impassioned."
Carolyn Heilbrun, *Writing a Woman's Life*.

he struggle of life in community forms a constant theme
in the vividly self-revealing autobiography of Abbess
Taisiia (1840–1915), a renowned educator and visionary.
It is only by the power of her writing and the honesty of her vision
that we feel the anguish she experienced throughout her life as she
saw the distressing gulf between her ideal—the monastic life—and
the fractious, often unedifying, everyday life of a convent. Gifted
with keen intellect, empowering visions, and formidable energy, she
aspired to the highest moral and spiritual standards for herself and
other religiously dedicated women. The spiritually vibrant communities she founded and shaped bear testimony to her impassioned
belief in women's religious capacity.

Difficulties and disagreements blend throughout Taisiia's life with luminous moments of joy and grace. Her parents were both of old noble families: her mother from the Pushkin family of Moscow, and her father from the Salopivs of St. Petersburg. In her autobiography, Taisiia describes her mother's great unhappiness in marriage: her shock as a young girl of sixteen, still devoted to her nanny, of being married to a cold and severe husband and her despair on losing two children in childbirth. Desperately seeking consolation from an unhappy marriage in motherhood, her mother prayed feverishly to the Mother of God for a child who would survive; when in 1840 a healthy young daughter was born to her, she named her, in gratitude, Mariia. Writing her autobiography at the age of sixty, Taisiia (Mariia) describes herself as "this God-granted daughter of a sorrowful mother."[1]

Mariia and her mother were inseparable. As a young girl, she sat on a little bench at her mother's knee, listening to her mother tell stories, mostly "about events in Sacred History, especially about the sufferings of the Savior." Mariia was also very precocious: at the age of four she could read and showed signs of a remarkable memory, having learned by heart most of the stories told to her.[2] Her childhood was spent under the supervision of a pious mother and a governess, who later prepared her for admission, at the age of ten, to the Pavlovsky Institute for Young Noble Women in St. Petersburg. When the time came for her to be delivered to the institute, her mother was so upset that she could not bear to go with her; her father took her there, blessed her, and departed, leaving her in tears. Her homesickness was intense and interfered with her ability to concentrate. As she later explained, "Remembering everything dear to heart that was now in the past and would never return, deprived me of the calmness necessary for study. Only because of my natural gifts was I able, after having read through my homework only once, to repeat it and keep up with my class."[3] But her health and spirits began to give way. She suffered terrible headaches and an inflamed eye, which became so severe that she temporarily lost her vision. Her parents, who with the coming of spring had moved to their country estate, were for some reason not informed of this, and her blindness continued well into autumn. Finally, an eye specialist was called, she was transferred to an eye clinic, and her parents were notified of her condition. When treatments resulted in no improvement, they took her to their country estate, where she gradually regained her vision. By the end of the year, she was able to return to the institute, but for the rest of her life, she had poor vision and it was extremely difficult for her to read by lamplight. She was forbidden to study during evening hours or to strain her eyes during the day. Nonetheless, she was one of the best pupils, for, as she explained, "Having deprived me of good outward vision, the Lord sharpened even more my inner understanding and memory. I was forced to rely on this for my education, rather than on my textbooks."[4] In class she listened intently to every word that was said, committed it to memory, and was able afterward to repeat it word for word to her classmates and help them with their homework. Her precociousness and her piety earned for her various nicknames, including "The Blind Wise One," "The Nun," "The Abbess," and, when she had particularly displeased someone, "The Sanctimonious Hypocrite." After a vision at the age of twelve, she was called "The Odd One."

When she was in sixth grade (age twelve), an epidemic of measles spread through the institute right before Easter. Feverish and in the infirmary, Mariia awoke from a sleep on Bright Night (Holy Saturday) to hear a kind of rustle, like the rustling of birds' wings. As she later recalled:

> I opened my eyes, and to my astonishment, I clearly and distinctly saw, in the dead of night, some kind of sunlit, winged being, flying beneath the ceiling and repeating with a human voice: "Christ is

risen! Christ is risen!" What this being was like I cannot tell, except that I saw something like a child's head beneath two little wings. Oh! What an unearthly joy my childish soul felt! It was as if something hitherto unknown to it, something sweet, came into it and subjugated it completely.

The feeling of sweetness remained with her for the rest of her life. It was as if that feeling was "the beginning of something new, something mysterious," which was unclear to her at the time.[5]

This experience prepared her for a major, life-changing vision, which occurred the following August, after she received Holy Communion during the Feast of the Dormition (the assumption of the Mother of God into heaven). She saw herself kneeling in a meadow covered with green grass, praying to God. The meadow was bordered by a forest, and about forty feet away, there was a long river flowing. On the opposite bank of that river was a big, noisy city, which, never having seen any other city, she took to be St. Petersburg. Hearing the loud noises, shouts, and talk coming from this city, she felt blessed to have come over to the other side of the river, to a peaceful and solitary meadow. Suddenly, she began to rise from the ground. She was flying higher and higher until finally, having reached a great height, she stopped ascending. She was in another world, in heaven. An indescribable sweetness filled her soul, and everything was so filled with light and beauty that she was powerless to express it, even later in recollection.

Close to her, a great number of human beings stood in long rows. The bodies of these beings were all the same, but "they were not coarse and rough like our earthly bodies." Instead, they were fine and transparent, so transparent that one could see through the first row to the next, and so on till the end of the innumerable rows. Some were in shades of yellow, others of red, blue, white, and so on, but all were light and transparent. At one point she looked at their bodies and thought, "Have I not become like them," but realized that neither her appearance nor her position had changed; she was still in her school uniform, and still on her knees, in aerial space. She looked down and saw the earth below and became alarmed at the thought of having to return there, when everything on high was "transparent and clear, without any trace of coarseness or materiality." The holy beings were arranged as though in two choirs, with a bright empty space between them. They sang beautifully, and a sweet fragrance came from their mouths. From her position at the beginning of the two rows, she could see far away into the empty space; she thought that over there was "the Throne of God, the Source of Light, and that He Himself was dwelling there." As soon as this thought came to her, one of the holy beings approached her and answered her thought, saying, "You want to see the Lord; you do not have to go anywhere, into the far distance. The Lord is here, all around us. He is always with us and at your side." When she wondered to herself who he was and how he could perceive her thoughts, he answered, without her having to speak, that he was the evangelist Matthew. He had scarcely finished saying this when, at her right side, facing her, she saw "our Savior, Jesus Christ." As she later wrote of this vision:

> It is frightful to begin to describe His divine sight; I know that nothing, no words can express this, and I fear lest a feeble human word belittle the Great One. It is impossible to remember, let alone describe, the divine, majestic appearance of the most sweet Lord, without tender emotion and trembling. Scores of years have passed since the day of that vision, but it is always there in my soul, alive and indelible![6]

When she awoke from this vision, tears were streaming down her face, and she asked to see a priest to help her interpret it. When she had told him everything, he kissed her on the forehead, assuring her that this was a calling from God and that she should keep it a secret until the Lord himself would complete his work. After this, as she says, it became easier for her to associate with people, but her "life-time choice was made; I felt a kind of tightness in my soul. I realized that it was impossible for me to live a conventional life."[7]

From her autobiography, memoirs of conversations, and letters of instructions she wrote to young nuns, it is clear that this vision marked her for life. The imagery remained with her constantly: of a God of light, a God enthroned; of transformed human beings with all coarseness gone; of a heaven on high; and of a higher life. Throughout her life, she struggled to be worthy to live the higher life and to ascend to that beautiful place, and she devoted a great deal of energy to inspiring others to the same goal. Part of her struggle would be to learn how to structure her life and then fight for the right to live by that structure so that she could be more open to graced moments such as her vision. She hoped that such moments could become the essence of her life rather than episodic experiences.

In her autobiography, she prefaced the chapter on this vision with the biblical quote: "If ye then be risen with Christ, seek those things which are above . . . for ye are dead, and your life is hid with Christ in God" (Col 3:1,3).[8] One of the things she felt dead to was the pleasures of the world, minimal as they were in the disciplined atmosphere of the institute. Having become indifferent to everything except the holy Gospel, she found herself often embarrassed and the object of school-girl teasing. When she took part in entertainments, usually involuntarily, she would become

> so confused, so ashamed of myself, remembering the heavenly beauty I had seen, feeling the true sweetness of spiritual delights. I would become unable to dance, participate in plays, or do anything of the sort. I would be lost, confused, sometimes even on the verge of tears, which would occasion general astonishment, and even laughter.[9]

During parties or dancing lessons, she began to feel dizzy and stagger until she received permission to avoid these activities altogether.

During these times she would sit alone and read spiritual literature or, somewhat sanctimoniously, pray for her classmates, whom she felt were not entirely without sin in their love of entertainment.

She sailed through her classes, devoting a minimum amount of time to her homework so she would be free for more introspective activities such as spiritual reading, fasting, and writing down her reflections and impressions. She found her Russian teachers more sympathetic to her fasting and religiosity than her German teachers, who were Lutheran. As she grew older, merely reading of edificatory books no longer satisfied her, especially as she had very few available to her. She loved, instead, the Gospel, finding in it such sweetness and comfort that she developed a "strange need to have these words always with me and never be separated from them."[10] So she decided to undertake what most people would consider a prodigious task: memorizing the Gospels and the Epistles of the New Testament by heart!

At the end of her senior year, the rector of the St. Petersburg Theological Academy came to examine the graduates in their religious studies. Having been told by Baroness Fredericks, the headmistress of the institute, that Mariia knew the Gospels by heart, he asked her to recite several long passages, which she did flawlessly, as her classmates rolled their eyes and looked at each other. Then he asked her what induced her to learn the whole Gospel by heart, which he said was rather unusual among young ladies of such an institute. She replied earnestly that she found every word of the Gospels so comforting that she always wanted to have them with her, but since it was not always convenient to have a book in one's hand, she had decided to memorize them. This elicited another exchange of glances from those assembled. Finally, he asked her to interpret the meaning of several passages of the Bible, which she did with great skill. It is interesting, and consistent with her belief in a higher life, that she interpreted Christ's commandment to "go sell what one has and give to the poor" as not being meant literally for all people but only for those wishing to lead a more perfect life.[11]

As graduation approached, Mariia realized with dread that, although she had been secretly looking forward for six years to the time when she could enter the more perfect life, which she understood to be the monastic life, her parents had entirely different plans for her. Her mother swooped down before graduation with a dressmaker and a milliner to prepare the obligatory long white dress for the December graduation and a host of other dresses for the parties and social season she envisioned for her daughter. She was bubbling over with the good news that Mariia had been left a sizable inheritance of property and money by her grandfather. When Mariia seemed saddened, even displeased, with all of this, her mother said impatiently, "What's wrong with you, Mashenka? You seem not to love us anymore! Have you become so serious?" After her mother left, she became profoundly thoughtful. There was indeed a lot to think over:

> I could see and feel that my dear, kind mother, who during my childhood and adolescence had had me for her only comfort, as I have said before, had during all these years of separation cherished the hope that when I completed my studies I would again become her only comfort, her only friend, the prop of her weakening health, her happiness, her pride, and so on. All of a sudden her sweet dreams would be shattered! And who would be to blame? It would be I, her infinitely beloved daughter![12]

There is perhaps something inflated in this account, since a son and a daughter had been born to her parents later in life, and thus Mariia was not the only source of her mother's happiness. But there nonetheless was a powerful bond forged between mother and daughter during Mariia's first ten years, a bond which she felt she now had to break in some way in order to fulfill the calling she felt so strongly. She grieved over the anguish she would cause her mother, and after a sleepless night, got up to pray, holding a small icon of "our Savior, Whose image as I had seen Him in heaven came vividly to my mind." Kissing the icon, with trembling lips, she cried aloud, "Could I betray you O most sweet Jesus? Is it possible that love for my mother, an earthly love, can be stronger than love for You? Oh, let it not be so! Never! Never!"[13]

Mariia resolved to tell her mother the next time she saw her that she felt unable to lead a worldly life and had a deep longing to enter a convent. When she did so, her mother looked aghast and asked her to never again repeat those words if she did not want to send her to her grave. A priest advised Mariia to wait patiently and trust that the Lord would not leave his work unfinished; he advised her not to enter a convent without her mother's blessing, as this would be displeasing to God.

So Mariia bided her time, allowing her mother, who by then had moved permanently with her ailing husband and two young children to their estate in the Borovichskii district of Novgorod province, to come to St. Petersburg and drag her through the social season of holiday balls and parties and outings to the opera and the theater. The parties, and the vapid conversation that went with them, particularly bored her; on the whole, she found all these city entertainments tedious, "not only worthless, but also empty, unable to give satisfaction to a serious person's mind."[14] When they returned to their country estate, which she hoped would be quieter, she found a similar whirl of social activity, as bored gentry visited each other for days on end to pass away the long Russian winter. The nearest church was three miles away, and services were conducted only on feast days; she missed the sacramental life the institute had provided. When summer finally came, she was relieved because "the idle life of the landowners gave way to a more active one. They now had work to do." On the pretext of having a closer look at the management of the farm, she asked her mother for permission to supervise the work in the fields. In between this supervising work, she would secretly read her spiritual books. These moments of stolen solitude gave her great satisfaction. She prayed that the Lord might free her from "this worldly bustle," which was becoming more unbearable to her each day. Fearing that with the coming of autumn the parties and idle pastimes would begin again, she worked out a plan to move to the house she had inherited from her grandfather in the town of Borovichi. She was not above using a few wiles to get her way. As she herself admitted: "I worked out the following way of life for myself. It could not be arranged without using a little stratagem. I used it!"[15]

What she did was to move to Borovichi with her brother, Konstantin, who was then eleven, on the grounds that it would be easier for him to study there and that she herself would undertake his preparation for entrance to a military academy. Her parents engaged two sisters from an impoverished gentry family, the Moskvins, to live rent free in two upstairs rooms of the house, but basically Mariia was able to do as she wished. Each morning she got up at dawn to attend matins at the local monastery, returning in time to awaken her brother, have breakfast with him, and begin their lessons at nine. She avoided all social invitations, though she received many, particularly as word got around that the heiress of the late General Vasilevskii had graduated from the institute and come to town. She also received requests to tutor many children, as there was at that time no public school in Borovichi for girls. Jealous of her time, she agreed to teach only three little girls from gentry families and a boy, as companion to her brother. She used the money from the lessons for charitable purposes. (Her mother had taken over control of her inheritance, since she was still under twenty-one.) She gave away many of her fine clothes and lived simply and happily, spending the evenings in reading and needle-work with the Moskvin sisters, who were fortunately very devout. But she still felt the calling to enter a convent, which meant that she was still on a collision course with her mother. When her mother found out that Mariia had given away an expensive pair of earrings for the support of a monastery on Mount Athos, she made a terrible scene. "Such occurrences and other similar ones grieved me," Mariia later wrote. "I saw them as a restriction on my free-dom, on my spiritual and moral aspirations. I came to the logical conclusion that I would never free myself from these restrictions until I would enter a convent."[16]

The battle to receive permission from her mother to enter a con-vent was painful. Her mother still hoped that Mariia would marry, have children, and live near her. Mariia secretly sought advice about her situation from Father Benjamin of the Borovichi monastery and Father Lavrentii, archimandrite of the Iveron monastery, who later became her spiritual director. Like Anastasiia, Matrona, and An-gelina, she was urged to patiently wait on God. One late November afternoon, she broke down in tears with her mother, telling her that although she was doing all she could to be obedient, she nonethe-less was "doing it all by force. It is very hard for me to go on living in the world. I am in agony, like a bird in a cage." Her mother lis-tened to her sobs and, in a moment of tenderness mixed with exas-peration, told her that if she really had so little regard for her family and home, she could go enter a convent but she should keep in mind that she would find there "no loving mother, dear family or your own home."[17]

Mariia moved quickly to bring her dreams to pass. She spent Christmas in the Iveron monastery and the rest of the holidays at the Tikhvin convent. It was her first visit to a convent and she felt an instant bond with the sisters. "All the faces of the nuns were so open, so friendly, that involuntarily the words of the Scriptures came to my mind: 'This is my resting place; here shall I dwell.'" She eagerly discussed with the abbess the possibility of entering this convent and returned to Borovichi filled with plans to sell her townhouse and settle her estate.[18] Her mother, meanwhile, had reverted to her former position of opposition, which crushed Mariia. Angry at Mariia's plans to sell her house, she said sarcastically:

> You might as well sell the house. You probably moved into it so as to be able to move around as you like, visiting churches and convents. When you won't have your house any longer, you will have to come back to the estate with us. It will be easier to dissipate your holiness, your neurosis, that way.[19]

Mariia lost all hope. But her break came, miraculously she believed, when her mother had a dream, the same night that Mariia did, that the Mother of God was calling Mariia to her. In her mother's dream was also a voice scolding her for refusing to let Mariia enter the convent; she awoke troubled, went to see Archimandrite Lavrentii to discuss the whole situation, and prayed to the Mother of God for guidance. In the end, she relented, and gave Mariia her long-withheld permission.[20]

After settling her estate, Mariia spent three days at the Iveron monastery, where Father Lavrentii helped prepare her for entry into the convent. He warned her against ascetic feats, perceptively predicting that for her, achieving humility and obedience would be greater and more difficult than any dramatic ascetic stunt. He emphasized that communal life was the best teacher of humility and warned her that because of the continual contact with others in a convent, clashes would inevitably ensue. "Here," he said, "is where you can find an occasion to demonstrate humility, by enduring sorrows and giving complete obedience, not only to superiors, but also to your equals and even to those under you." She had reason many times to remember these words as she later felt the rub of communal life.

Father Lavrentii also instructed her in the importance of inner prayer, telling her to pray continuously with her "inner mind," the deeper mind that Orthodoxy cherished. He asked her to remember that her vocation was a great gift, something she had not merited; since she had been gifted in many ways, much would be expected of her. She took to heart his biblical reminder, "From him to whom much is given will much be required" (Lk 12:48); her later writings abound with an acute sense of responsibility and accountability, particularly during her thirty-four years as head of the Leushino community. In parting, Father Lavrentii kissed her on the head, called her "little lamb," gave her a prayer rope he had used to train himself in continual prayer, and promised to pray perpetually for her. Mariia was very moved by his love and understanding, finding it harder to part from him than from her own family:

> This parting from a man so spiritually close to me, who understood all the strivings and movements of my soul, who had come to me so lovingly and warmly when (as it seemed to me) the whole world had turned its back on me as though I were demented—this parting from a man to whom I was indebted for my whole subsequent life was much harder to endure than the parting from my parents, or with everything seemingly "my own."[21]

The convent Mariia entered was called the Convent of the Entry of the Mother of God into the Temple, or the Vvedenskii Tikhvinskii women's monastery.[22] It was located in the town of Tikhvin, in Novgorod province, across the river from the "Great Monastery" of Tikhvin, a men's monastery. The abbess, Mother Seraphima, was a learned, kind person who came from high society. Before entering the convent, Mariia went to see her to discuss financial arrangements. Mariia had heard from the sisters that novices from gentry families were often unable to cope with the hard monastic obediences and work and therefore often made a monetary contribution on entry so that they would not be a burden to the community.

Mariia asked Mother Seraphima to suggest the amount of contribution she should make and was surprised when the abbess replied:

> You do not have to make any contribution. Persons like you are themselves an asset to the convent, for only a few come to us. You can be useful to us, being a gifted and educated girl. Besides, you have a command of both singing and music. We are teaching this especially to young peasant girls, not having any educated ones on hand.

She did suggest, however, that Mariia keep some money for personal expenses, such as garments, tea, and other incidentals.[23] In the end, Mariia brought seven hundred rubles with her to the convent, asking the abbess to take three hundred rubles out of this total as her contribution. Seraphima said she would keep the whole sum for her in a safe place and would twice a year give her the interest it earned, which amounted to seventeen rubles. As it turned out, Mariia needed this allowance, as the only thing she had been given free was her cell, firewood, and, according to her, "a meager fare." Everything else had to be obtained at her own expense: "tea, sugar, a piece of white bread to eat with our tea, if needed (and with our meager fare it certainly was), our outer clothing (*podraznik*), plates and dishes, the samovar," everything needed for daily life including the coal and kindling for the samovar. "Under these conditions, Mariia "came to lack everything." She later recalled: "Keeping in mind my elder's instructions, I bore all these privations without murmuring; however, human weakness made itself felt."[24] The Spartan character of monastic life was becoming a reality for her.

She was immediately assigned to the choir, to sing and to read in church. As a first-year novice, she was also assigned to all communal duties and services, including work in the fields and the kitchen. She particularly disliked washing the plates and dishes following the communal meal. After washing about two hundred plates, dishes, and spoons, her hands would be bleeding from the lye solution. If she so much as mentioned it, "a shower of mockery and caustic remarks" were poured on her. She had great difficulty adjusting to the variety of hard tasks and, as Father Lavrentii had predicted, to obedience itself. In her autobiography, she complains:

> They forced me to do all kinds of incidental work, without asking of course, "Can you do it?," "Do you know how to do it?," "Are you capable of doing it?," "Do you have enough strength to do it?," etc. It was just one word: "Obedience does not calculate," "Obedience does not contradict"; they order to do something, and you do it, saying, "bless me."[25]

For a young woman who had taken great pride in being at the top of her class, it seems that she was particularly galled at being exposed as incompetent or unskilled at several of the tasks essential to the community. Obedience led her into humbling situations; it would teach her, as all monastics learn, the grit of humility.

At the end of the first year, Mariia was assigned to a teaching position. The town of Tikhvin had requested the convent to open a preparatory course for girls, as no such school existed in the city. Mariia was delighted by this challenging assignment and relieved to give up her work in the fields and the kitchen. Her daily schedule now consisted of getting up at 4:00 A.M., for matins, then having tea and preparing for classes, which began at 9:00. Classes continued until noon, at which point she ate lunch in the refectory. From 1:00 to 4:30 P.M., classes continued, with a break for a walk. She went immediately from classes to vespers, after which she stayed to hear the monastic rule (the set prayers of the convent). Only at 8:00 P.M. did she return to her cell, exhausted and ready for tea.

One of her pupils was A. Snetkova, the daughter of a wealthy Tikhvin timber merchant whose parents began to make substantial donations to the convent after she started studying there. Thus,

Mariia's teaching, as she proudly noted, "was not a negligible asset
to the convent. This gave me great joy. The Mother Superior as well
as the older nuns always showed me their gratitude and goodwill."
On one occasion, however, the Snetkovs' pleasure with Mariia
caused her great distress. On January 25, the eve of Mariia's name
day, A. Snetkova handed Mariia a letter from her father, saying that
the family would come by tomorrow to celebrate her name day. She
also gave Mariia an envelope, which Mariia opened only later that
night. In it, to her consternation, she found a twenty-five ruble note,
evidently intended as a name-day gift. Mariia told the abbess about
it the next morning before matins. The abbess was pleased with
Mariia's openness and honesty and told her to keep the money for
her own use; she also told the elder nuns about it. Word soon spread
about the gift, leading to jealousy and rumors about Mariia. Always
sensitive to slight, she took these rumors badly, viewing them as
calumny and affliction. She was particularly distressed at the nega-
tive reaction of some of the older sisters, who just shortly before had
been so pleased with her. Although she tried to bear her suffering
with resignation, her active, critical mind kept asking questions like:
"Why are those in authority so short-sighted as to be unable to discern truth from falsehood? Why are they so quickly inclined to
trample down that which, not so long ago, occasioned them tenderness and concern?" Or even more troubling: "Where can one
find truth when it is absent even in its representatives?" Even after
the storm had passed and she had regained everyone's kindness and
esteem, she reflected on the injustice and fickleness of people's feelings. As she later recalled in her autobiography: "My soul had been
profoundly shocked, and it could not be easily calmed. In place of
my former cheerful and happy manner, I became mistrustful, sorrowful, and suspicious." Having personally experienced it, she
could not help realizing "that all this love and kindness could as

quickly be changed to wicked and venomous mockery as one hour follows another."[26]

Fortunately, the convent also provided times of great spiritual sustenance for Mariia. One such moment, which she recalled with great significance in her autobiography, was an unexpected opportunity to witness the "fervent, meaningful prayer of an aged nun." It happened that she was sent on an errand to a very old nun, Mother Feokfista. On coming to her cell, she recited the Jesus prayer aloud, as is the customary greeting in monasteries. There was no answer. Supposing that Mother Feokfista had not heard her; she opened the door just a little and repeated the prayer, this time somewhat louder. Again no answer. Having said the Jesus prayer for the third time, she entered the cell and was unable to make another move, being struck with reverence and surprise by what she saw. Mother Feokfista was on her knees in a corner of her room, with her arms uplifted. Her lips were moving and her face was wet with tears, which were also streaming down her clothes. Every now and then she prostrated herself and remained for a long time in that position. Only her sobs showed her state. Mariia recalled with awe:

> I felt ill at ease for having entered the room. Involuntarily I had become a witness of the inner secret of an aged nun's soul. It had taken me quite unawares—or could it have been an indication from the Lord, Who was showing me this either to give me a lesson on prayer, or to shatter my doubts as to whether there were any old nuns in our convent who were leading a high spiritual life?

Mariia stood still, fearing to move lest she disturb the old nun's prayer and afraid to leave without having accomplished her errand. She had to wait for more than an hour before Feokfista began to rise from her knees. Mariia was at first afraid to tell her that she had witnessed her prayerful ecstasy, but finally broke into tears at what she had seen. After a beautiful, soul-to-soul talk, Feokfista asked her not to tell anyone what she had seen. Mariia kept it to herself, but the incident brought her great spiritual benefit. She had seen how nuns prayed, and she began trying to emulate them.[27]

In February of the fourth year of her stay in the convent, she received a letter from her mother saying that she was seriously ill and begging Mariia to come home. Her mother asked plaintively, "If I die, who will take care of your young sister, not to mention the house and the whole estate in general?" Mariia was particularly unnerved by her mother's concluding words: "Stay, I beg you! Take care of the house and the orphans. For their sake do not let the estate dwindle away into alien hands!" Mariia was afraid that if she went home, her mother would ask her to give up her life in the convent. (Since she had not yet been tonsured and taken final vows, this was legally possible.) She suffered terrible torment, not knowing if she could stand firm against such a request from her mother on her deathbed. She knew she needed to ask someone for advice, but her heart warned her that she would be advised to go. In deep conflict, she asked the abbess, who told her that she could not advise her; Mariia would have to do what she thought right. Finally, she asked permission to visit the miraculous icon of Our Lady of Tikhvin at the "Great Monastery" where she would pray for guidance. Sobbing, she begged the Mother of God to show her "the best way to act, so that the result would benefit my soul, and not this transient life." She kept putting off writing to her mother, knowing that it would sadden her if she refused to come. Suddenly, on March 19 she received a telegram informing her that her mother had passed away on March 17 and that her presence was urgently needed.

She left immediately for home, where she found chaos, an invalid will, no trustee for the estate, and no provision for her sister, Klavdiia, who was then twelve. She spent the next five months straightening out the estate. She traveled to St. Petersburg to beg for her sister's entry into Pavlovsky Institute, which she herself had attended, and arranged scholarships for both her sister's and brother's schooling. Then she spent the summer preparing her sister, whose tutoring had been neglected during her mother's illness, for her entry into the institute in the fall. Although she was clearly capable and effective, she found this time of "living in the world" a great moral strain. It was with great delight that she returned at the end of August to her beloved convent.[28]

Since the Tikhvin convent, unlike women's religious communities (*zhenskie obshchiny*) and the communal convents that developed from them, was juridically a noncommunal (*neobshchezhitel'nyi*) convent, the nuns "owned" the cells in which they lived; that is they had been bought for life by their inhabitants. As Mariia explained it, "all the repairs and the maintenance of the cell become the responsibility of the owner. She lives in it as a full-fledged housewife. According to her own discretion, she chooses a novice to live with her and to do the house chores." The poorer nuns who could not afford to "buy" a cell had to live in the common quarter—that is, wherever and with whomever they could find a place. The Tikhvin convent followed this practice of noncommunal convents except that cells were supposed to be "sold" only to those who had lived at the convent for a certain length of time. Mariia decided, on her return from her family's estate, that she wanted to buy a cell of her own; Father Lavrentii, whom she had visited while home, had encouraged her to do so. When she asked the abbess to give her a cell and offered money for it, the abbess replied that she could have a cell in the new building that had been completed during the summer but that she did not have to give money for it since the wood for the building had been supplied by the timber merchant Snetkov, who had expressly asked that a cell in the building be reserved for Mariia. So Mariia moved into a lovely corner cell on the second floor of the new building, a bright and airy apartment with windows to the south and east. Being only twenty-six and still a novice, she thought that an older nun might be assigned to live with her, but instead she was given a cell attendant and a young girl from St. Petersburg, Luba Kolesnikova. Mariia lived in the back room; Luba and the cell attendant, in the front. The cell attendant was busy all day with different obediences, and Luba and Mariia, both members of the choir, attended all the church services and occupied themselves the rest of the day with needlework in their respective cells. Now that "neither business nor the presence of undesirable people" could distract her, Mariia firmly resolved with God's help to begin accustoming herself to inner prayer and self-concentration. She gave herself over completely to this task and corresponded freely with Father Lavrentii about her spiritual progress. This was the best and happiest time of her life:

> If I have ever gained anything for my inner self, it is all due to that period. My inner life went so calmly that I didn't even dare hope it would last long. I saw my state not as "life on the Cross" (in the monastic sense), but rather as "life in Paradise," if ever Paradise can be attained here on earth. I experienced the force of Christ's words, "The Kingdom of God is within you."

In this cell, for the first time, she also experienced something like what she witnessed with Mother Feokfista.[29]

She lived for several years in her "priceless little cell." During her first year in it, she received the "little" tonsure and was made a ryassaphore nun. She also received the name of Arkadiia, since not long before, the candle maker, Arkadiia, had passed away and they wished to perpetuate her memory in the convent. After six years of calm and peace in this nurturing cell, a terrible trial befell her: Luba's stepmother wished to enter the convent and offered the abbess an eight-hundred-ruble contribution for Arkadiia's cell. The abbess wished to accept the eight hundred rubles, considering it a "substantial morsel" for the convent. Understanding what monastic obedience required, Arkadiia offered to leave her cell but was completely dismayed to find that all that was available was a stone-walled cell located on the ground floor, where there was constant dampness and flooding in the spring. She was so upset that she could hardly move, and staggered out of the abbess's office, with a flood of angry thoughts rushing through her head:

> Didn't she tell me herself that she held my work in high esteem? Didn't she tell me that the Snetkovs, who erected this building, had asked her expressly to give me a cell in it? Didn't she refuse the money I had offered several times as a contribution to the convent for my cell? Hadn't she received thousands of rubles for my work teaching the children—donations of money, flour, household utensils, timber, everything thinkable! Where is justice? Where is human love? Why, to send a girl of noble, tender upbringing to such a damp cell!

But move she must. Her new dwelling consisted of two subdivisions. The first one was completely dark, so Luba and the cell attendant could do nothing in it except sleep. They therefore worked in Arkadiia's room, which had two small windows. The entire wall under these windows from one corner to the other was covered with mold for nearly a yard. The air was unbearably stale and gave them constant headaches. The winter spent in that cell left a permanent mark on Mariia's health. Frequently sick, she could no longer sing in the choir or do the readings in church. When a friend visited in July, she was shocked at Arkadiia's appearance and the moldy walls. Being a friend of Father Lavrentii's, she reported Mariia's situation to him. He wrote her a letter, saying categorically that if she were not out of the cell by winter, it would constitute a valid reason for moving to another convent. But Arkadiia, who had been at the Tikhvin convent for fourteen years, had misgivings about leaving. As she said, it "was the cradle of my monastic life; here had elapsed the best, as well as the most painful, of my spiritual endeavors." Her dilemma was momentarily solved when she was summoned in the beginning of November to the Novgorod Provincial Chamber in connection with her grandfather's estate. The abbess encouraged her to stay in Novgorod through the winter, promising to prepare a more comfortable cell for her in the spring. But as she left, she and the older nuns had a premonition that she would not return; they parted in tears.[30]

Her first visit in Novgorod was to Father Lavrentii. He assured her that what she had suffered had a purpose: she had to bear this cross in order to become more spiritual. She was beginning the painful process of learning selfless patience; he believed that she had much more to learn in this area but that God would help her. In the meantime, he advised her to look over the four convents in the city of Novgorod and choose the one that appealed to her most. When she did, she was shocked by the lack of cloistering in most of them. In the Holy Spirit convent, there were not even common meals, so the nuns had to prepare their own, which often caused them to miss the liturgy. In the end, she settled in the Zverin Protection of the Mother of God Convent (Pokrovskii Zverin), partly through the initiative of the abbess who, being a connoisseur of good singing, was eager to have Arkadiia.[31]

Arkadiia was promptly appointed leader of the right choir, a stressful duty because of the abbess's exacting standards and the difference in melodies between the Zverin convent and the Tikhvin convent. During this time, she wrote the words and music for an *akathist* to St. Symeon the God Receiver, which was approved by the Synod and became part of the official canon for his feast day.[32] But she also ran into some difficulties in the convent, which "came from the direction of those heading the administration." Maddeningly, she does not explain in her autobiography the nature of the difficulties for fear of leading her readers into temptation.[33]

She found the Zverin convent less disciplined than the Tikhvin convent and more filled with intrigues. She began to feel greatly discouraged that the monastic life as practiced differed so sharply from her ideals. Under these circumstances, life in community drained her. Her inner prayer had become so distracted that she began to fear for her soul:

> Be it as it may, I have already lost my salvation, and all my monastic labors have been in vain. Once I left behind my first convent where I was rooted, I will never be able to feel at ease in this one, whether because of its ambience, its numerous intrigues, or for any other reason. If I were to enter yet another convent, the same would happen, or worse. And what kind of a convent is this (or any of the others in the city)? The nuns have to make their own livings. They have no time for the "one thing needful"; they must perforce be "careful and troubled over many things." And how many sins they have against each other—unfriendliness, envy, pride. We are just pretending to be nuns here.

At times she felt that they were just fooling people; it would be better to leave the convent altogether and live in solitude, quietly achieving one's salvation.[34] When she complained to Father Lavrentii once about the laxity of the Novgorod convents, he told her that she was being too judgmental, that many nuns found salvation within these places.[35] So she was torn between her spiritual desire to be more humble and less judgmental and her critical mind, which observed many troubling things.

This tension is disturbingly evident in a dream she had, which is called in her autobiography "The High Path." She dreamed that she was walking along a road in an open field. She had to turn to the right, but there was no path in that direction, only beds for planting vegetables. The furrows between the beds were wet and dirty so that if she walked along them she would get dirty, but if she walked across the ridges, she would get caught in the mud. Suddenly, she saw an old bishop coming in her direction, with a staff in his hand. He guided her along the higher path, the ridges, saying "Although it's muddy and you will often get stuck, the path is high; look how much dirt and water there is along the low path." They walked together for a long time, and as he preached to her, she realized he was St. Nicholas. Finally, they came to a chapel that had a large crucifix and an icon of St. Paraskeva. She began to prostrate herself before the crucifix; as her head touched the floor, the holy man struck her on the neck with such force that she thought he would chop off her neck. He did this five times. She asked herself why he was beating her; did he really want to chop off her head? Why would he want to do that? "Don't argue, don't act wise," he said in answer to her thoughts. "If I struck you it was because I had to. You have forgotten that one must obey without arguing. You don't have to show off your knowledge." Then he smiled at her kindly, and as she stood up, pointed to the icon of St. Paraskeva, reminding her that Paraskeva, an early Christian martyr, had allowed her head to be cut off as an offering to her Bridegroom. He told Arkadiia, "You are unable to suffer even a little, and you keep on philosophizing while you still don't possess spiritual wisdom. Humble yourself; endure, and you will be saved."[36] As this dream reveals, Arkadiia was clearly wondering if she would really have to cut off her head, and her critical mind, in order to be saved.

At this troubling time in her life, Arkadiia received contradictory signs of whether her intelligence, education, and analytical abilities were appreciated. In 1878 she was transferred to the Zvanskii Convent of the Sign of the Mother of God (Zvanskii Znamenskii), where she was appointed treasurer (a position second in command to the abbess) and assistant director of the Derzhavin Diocesan School for Girls.[37] This indicated high regard for her abilities from the church authorities in Novgorod, who were responsible for the appointment. On the other hand, the abbess of the Zvanskii convent, who was of humble, uneducated background, resented Arkadiia, telling her she was vain if she did something well, incompetent if she did it imperfectly. Requiring her to concentrate on the most tedious aspects of bookkeeping, the abbess eventually had her removed from her position in the school, which Arkadiia considered a great waste of her education and talent.[38]

After a year at the Zvanskii convent, Arkadiia received the full tonsure and was given the monastic name of Taisiia, the name by which she is remembered.[39] In 1881, at the age of only forty, she was appointed mother superior of the Leushino community in the eastern part of Novgorod diocese. In her autobiography she says that in general this appointment was a surprise to her because of her age and the fact that she had only served as treasurer for a few years. But she had a specific premonition of the appointment the night before word of the promotion came. That evening, she dreamed that she was walking through a field of rye and noticed that the ears were overripe so the grains had fallen to the ground. She wondered what kind of master it was who would be so careless as to deprive himself of such a treasure by not harvesting it in time. At this, a voice answered, telling her that she was the one who would have to harvest the whole field. She became terrified, not even knowing how to harvest. She soon came to an enormous expanse of water and had trouble crossing it. The water became deeper and deeper, and she was afraid she might drown. Suddenly, from above, as if from the sky, an abbess's staff fell directly into her hand. The same voice that had told her about the rye said, "Lean on it, you will not drown." She walked on until she reached a green meadow in which there were a white convent and a church. As she approached, leaning on her abbatical staff, a procession was coming toward the church. The choir came up to her, chanting, "Meet it is . . . ," a solemn hymn sung to dignitaries and on special occasions. She entered the church with the procession, and there her dream ended.

When, as part of her monastic obedience, she openheartedly told the abbess about her dream the next morning, the abbess made fun of her, sarcastically replying, "Congratulations! Now that you have received a staff, you are already an abbess!" That afternoon, to her surprise, the abbess received a telegram from Metropolitan Isidor telling her that Taisiia was to be immediately sent to St. Petersburg in connection with her appointment as head of the Leushino community.[40]

Unbeknownst to her, Taisiia was stepping into a hornet's nest. Sources independent of Taisiia's autobiography indicate that the Leushino community was deeply troubled and had already run through several mothers superior prior to Taisiia's appointment in 1881.[41] The origins of the community go back to the late 1840s, when a government engineer, N. N. Kargopol'tsev, bought an estate in Leushino for his widowed mother. Being very devout, Mrs. Kargopol'tsev was distressed that the closest church was ten miles away; to make matters worse, the area was filled with swampy marshes and the roads were often impassable, particularly at Easter time during the spring thaw. Through great effort, the Kargopol'tsevs and the local peasants were able to get the resources and permission to build a parish church: the son donated a piece of land for a church and cemetery and lumber for the building; the peasants volunteered their labor; and Mrs. Kargopol'tsev, in spite of her old age, donned the sack of a pilgrim-wanderer, begging donations for the church. Finally, in October 1860, the foundation was laid in the name of St. John the Forerunner (John the Baptist). Following the abolition of serfdom in 1861, the Kargopol'tsevs' finances became greatly strained; in addition, Mr. Kargopol'tsev received a new appointment requiring his transfer to the Tver region. In 1869 they were forced to put their estate up for sale. Hearing of this, Mother Sergiia, a nun from the Holy Sophia women's monastery in Rybinsk who had known Mrs. Kargopol'tsev and had dreamed of starting a women's convent in the secluded village of Leushino, moved heaven and earth to find a benefactor to buy the Kargopol'tsev estate and donate it for the establishment of a convent. From her frequent pilgrimages to holy places, she had become acquainted with several well-to-do people, including the Maximovs, a St. Petersburg business family. She persuaded the Maximovs to buy the Kargopol'tsev land, which amounted to 2,160 acres at the cost of five thousand silver rubles. The problem now was how to start a convent.

Mother Sergiia knew six elderly virgins (*keleinitsy* or *spasennitsy*) in Voronits village, twenty-five miles from Leushino, who lived quietly and modestly in a special cell apart from society. She persuaded them to move to Leushino to begin a women's religious community. She could not herself undertake this task, because as a tonsured nun, she was forbidden from living on the property of lay people, which Leushino was considered until the time of its official recognition in 1875 as a "monastic community" (*zhenskaia obshchina*) by the Holy Synod. Mr. Maximov himself settled the women on the estate, appointed the oldest one to be in charge, fixed up the old landowner's house, and departed for St. Petersburg.

The women, all of peasant origin, were in constant need of money for food, horses, agricultural implements, and building supplies. Having donated the land, the Maximovs considered their financial obligations complete, although they did play a direct role, by correspondence, in the governing of the estate and hence of the community. The women worked and prayed, following the church typicon of nocturns, matins, and vespers. But because they were an unofficial community, living technically as tenants on someone else's property, the police often visited them, demanding proof of their right to be there and suspecting that they formed some sort of dubious sect.

Maximov typically came to their rescue by mail, assuring the police that procedures were underway to have the women who were living together on his property recognized as a women's religious community.

It was therefore with great joy that the first sisters of Leushino, living in dire need and in fear for the future, received the imperial confirmation on January 11, 1875, of the establishment of the Leushino monastic community for women (*zhenskaia obshchina*). Mother Sergiia, who was then sixty-seven, was appointed mother superior, an appointment that quickly exhausted her. She worried not only about the financial and physical well-being of the establishment, but also even more about its spiritual well-being. The sisters were used to their own ways and to having Maximov as their supervisor, whereas she wanted to introduce the moral and liturgical discipline of a well-ordered monastic community and to have her position of authority recognized. After nearly two years of wrangling with the community, she asked to be relieved of her duties and returned to the Holy Sophia convent in Rybinsk. A similar fate befell her successor, the nun Leontiia, who was transferred to Leushino from the Goritskii Ascension convent in 1877. Although she accomplished a great deal with the physical plant, renovating the church and building a refectory and a large dormitory, she also encountered interference in the internal management of the community; in 1881, she returned to her well-ordered Goritskii convent.[42]

According to Taisiia, when she went to see Metropolitan Isidor in February 1881 about her appointment to head the Leushino community, he told her that the community needed intelligent administration and active supervision, that it was running through mothers superior, and that if she could not do something with it, he would close it. He also warned her that she might be lonely, as it was in a remote corner, a wilderness.[43]

It was not the remoteness that bothered Taisiia but the interference of the Maximovs and the clique of sisters who ran to them about every change or order they disliked. With that air of condescension she at times unwittingly revealed, she attributed this problem in part to the fact that "being illiterate peasant girls, they completely lacked any notions of the standards of monastic life." But she thought that the most important feeling that governed them was envy: they had seniority in terms of the number of years they had been in the community and were irritated at being governed by some nun "coming from God Knows where."[44] As usual, spiritually empowering dreams fortified her for the trials ahead. Before setting out for Leushino, in a mood of great trepidation, she dreamed that the Mother of God was assuring her of her protection of the community, as was the living head of St. John the Baptist, which lay at Mary's feet. Another time, when she was just beginning to put the community into "good order" and encountering resistance, she dreamed that she saw a huge wooden cross standing on the floor and wondered how she would be able to lift it. She became frightened and crossed herself, murmuring, "How large it is! How will I be able to carry it?" Then she heard these comforting words, as if coming from the cross itself: "You *will* lift it and carry it, for My strength is made perfect in weakness!"[45]

Taisiia's crosses were indeed many during her early years at the community. A hard core of dissidents, numbering seven in a community of over forty, resented her efforts to deepen the spiritual life of the community. Defying her at every stage, they finally, in October of 1882, staged a surprise one day in the refectory by announcing that they were leaving the community and urging others to join them. No one else followed them, but they caused quite a stir. Taisiia duly wrote to the bishop, reporting the whole incident and asking him to give them official permission to leave the community. Being more experienced in these affairs, he advised her to make them sign a declaration that they were leaving the community voluntarily, after which he promised to send the necessary dismissal papers. When she asked them to sign the declaration, they refused. Leaving secretly in the dead of night with their possessions in tow, they then wrote to Metropolitan Isidor claiming that Taisiia had turned them out. The Maximovs also sent a letter to the metropolitan complaining about Taisiia's behavior. According to Taisiia, the Maximovs—having lost control of the community—were hoping that it would be closed and the property revert to them so they could open a cheese dairy on the land.

When Taisiia went to St. Petersburg for her annual report to the metropolitan, he showed her the letters of complaint and asked her to write a letter explaining the situation. Although he was sympathetic to her, she was so distressed by what she considered to be lies and slander that she almost fainted in the metropolitan's office. When she returned to the friends' apartment where she was staying in St. Petersburg, she fell into a state of paralysis. Her arms and legs became numb, and she literally could not move from bed. She remained at her friends' in that condition for two weeks and spent another five weeks in a hospital. By the end of this time she was beside herself with worry over the state of the sisters in Leushino, who she knew were anxious about her and troubled by unsettling rumors.[46]

Early one morning as she lay overwhelmed with anxiety, she began to cry bitterly. Suffering from paralysis and unable to wipe her face with a handkerchief, she turned her head and began wiping it on the pillow. Then, as she reports, "something extraordinary happened. It could not have happened in my sleep, for I was not sleeping. Maybe it happened in a kind of daze; otherwise, I am at a loss to explain it."[47] She felt strongly the presence of someone in the room with whom she was talking about her need to have an icon of the Archangel Michael. Just then a beautiful youth appeared, wearing a blue cassock and carrying an icon of the

Archangel Michael. She begged him to give her the icon, as her arms and legs were paralyzed and she could not get it for herself. Suddenly, she realized that the face on the icon and that of the warrior were identical. This confused her because the angel in the icon had on warrior's clothing and wielded a fiery sword, but here was a youth wearing a cassock, which seemed strangely inadequate. He assured her that despite his clothing, he was powerful as "the angels are the executors of the Heavenly Father's will." He then told her to go to her convent, as he would be with her. He repeated this three times, and each time she knelt down and kissed the icon. With the third blessing, she came to herself, lowered her legs from her bed, put on her clothing, and prepared for her journey back to Leushino. By that afternoon, she was on the train to Rybinsk, confident that the Archangel Michael had himself healed her and would be with her in her work at Leushino.[48]

Her work at Leushino seemed indeed to be blessed. The whole community calmed down, she was able to establish a spirit of deep prayer, work, and monastic discipline, and she built an impressive stone wall around the grounds to enhance the feeling of a cloister. Being deeply devoted to the sacramental life, she put great energy into the liturgical and aesthetic aspects of the church services. Her great love was liturgical music, and she trained a choir that became famous throughout the area and formed a source of great consolation every summer to Father John Sergiev (1829–1908), later canonized as St. John of Kronstadt, Russia's great saint of the twentieth century.[49]

When she had completed the stone wall in 1884, she invited the bishop of Novgorod to bless it, hoping he would also see how well the community was doing. Her plan succeeded: he spent three days visiting, talking with each sister and observing everything—the barns, cellars, stables, meadows, fields, and woods—and sent a glowing report to the metropolitan. On the basis of this, Taisiia dared to send a petition to the Synod asking that the Leushino community be elevated to the status of a monastery; this request was granted in September 1885, and in October Taisiia was given the title of abbess.

Having received the authorization to tonsure some of the sisters (a consequence of the community's being elevated to a monastery), Taisiia picked as the day of their tonsure November 8, the feast day of Archangel Michael and all the heavenly hosts. Her choice was made, as she explained, for two reasons: "(1) Monasticism being the angelic state, it is fitting to begin it on the day of its prototype; and (2) I am forever indebted to Archangel Michael, my Great Intercessor, for my healing and my subsequent work for the good of the community."[50] During the tonsuring service, she was overcome with joy. Her heart was palpitating, and as she led the choir in the beautiful chanting of the cherubic hymn, she fell into ecstasy. All of her senses were overpowered with the refrain, "Let us lay aside all earthly cares"; she looked upward and saw above the iconostasis the Savior himself surrounded by angels. She later described both the ecstasy and the consternation brought by this vision:

> Something was happening, but what it was I am unable to tell, although I saw and heard everything. It was something not of this world. From the beginning of the vision, I seemed to fall into ecstatic rapture. I have no idea how the choir finished the Cherubic Hymn, or how the Great Entrance took place: I saw and understood nothing. I do not even remember how the tuning fork passed from my hands into the choir-leader's. . . . Tears were streaming down my face. I realized that everyone was looking at me in astonishment, and even fear. They (i.e., the singers) probably thought I was not feeling well, for they began to ask what was the matter with me, why my countenance had changed, and they offered me a seat. To conceal my vision, I complied and sat down—and also in order to actually "come to my senses." What exactly I saw, or what happened to me, I am at a loss to explain.[51]

Empowered by visions like this, Taisiia strove throughout her thirty years as abbess to exalt the things she believed in passionately: the spiritual and sacramental life of the church and the education of its people. One of her most daunting enterprises was the construction of a stone church for the monastery, a project she undertook with only 240 rubles in hand and an architect's estimate of 180,000 silver rubles! To strengthen herself for this enterprise, she went on a pilgrimage to the great Monastery of the Caves in Kiev. As she wished to dedicate her church to the Mother of God, she prayed while in Kiev with special resonance to Mary and to St. Anthony, the eleventh-century founder of the Kiev monastery, who had also built a church dedicated to the Mother of God. She found his example still inspiring: "True, I pondered, times have changed, and so have people, and we who now build churches are far from being St. Anthony. However, God remains the same, without changing: He is the Almighty Builder for the good of his servants."

Once again fortified, she returned to Leushino and was able to oversee, within three years' time, the construction of a magnificent temple, the glory of the region, a project built almost entirely through "widows' mites," since she never received a whole thousand-ruble bill as a donation, and very few hundred-ruble bills.[52] She also founded at Leushino a parish school for local children and a school for the orphan daughters of clergymen. (In Orthodoxy, parish priests, as opposed to monks, are able to marry.) Although it began at the elementary level, under her energetic leadership the monastery expanded to include a teacher's training institute, an ecclesiastical college for girls.[53] This was a remarkable accomplishment for a backwoods area like Leushino, the equivalent of building an institution of higher education in the mountains of Appalachia or a remote region of Montana. The administration of Leushino and the spiritual direction of the nuns and novices also challenged

Taisiia's energy. According to a monastic survey of Russia taken in 1907, the Leushino St. John the Forerunner women's monastery had over 2,100 acres of land, an abbess, fifty-seven nuns, and forty novices.[54]

Taisiia considered the instruction of novices in the ways of monastic life among her most important duties. Gifted in this, she trained nuns not only for Leushino, but also for a host of other communities she helped found along with John of Kronstadt, including Surskii Ioanno-Bogoslovskii in Arkhangelsk province, Vorontsovskii Glagoveshchenskii in Pskov province, and Ioannovskii Karpovkskii in St. Petersburg.[55] The fruit of all of this teaching was contained in her *Letters to Beginning Nuns About the Most Important Responsibilities of the Monastic Life*, which was first published in 1900.[56] The book was so popular and beneficial that the Holy Synod reprinted it several times and distributed it to all monasteries and *sketes* and to many parishes, making it a main guidebook for female monastic aspirants.[57] If we consider that in 1907 there were 448 women's monasteries and monastic communities in the Russian Empire with a total of 66,000 nuns and novices, we have an idea of the extent of her influence in shaping the spiritual life of Russian monastic women in the years before the Russian Revolution.[58]

It is notable that the subtitle to her book indicates that it is "Composed on the basis of the ascetic writings of the Holy Fathers, the examples of the Holy Fathers, and my own experience of many years." The authority of her own experience in faith, prayer, and inner struggle surges through the book, giving it a powerful freshness and immediacy. At the same time, her extensive reading of patristic literature, primarily of the ascetic works, is apparent, as is her legendary knowledge of the Bible.

The book is arranged in the form of fourteen letters on various topics including the origins of monasticism, obedience to spiritual elders (*staritsy*), the novitiate, mutual love, mental prayer, and the inevitability of suffering. The first letter welcomes the newly ar- rived aspirants to the monastic life and emphasizes here, as throughout the book, the importance of love. She advises them, as they stand on the threshold of monastic life, to begin with love. Love is higher than all external ascetic exploits, and without love all righteous acts are meaningless. She urges them to do things that we know she struggled to learn how to do: to guard themselves against judging others, serve all, consider themselves worse than all, preserve love for all in their hearts, and express it. In loving their neighbor, they will find a miraculous peace, sweet and grati- fying.[59]

The second letter contains a brief, though learned, sketch of the origins of monasticism and communal life as well as many examples of ascetic figures from early church history. Taisiia is careful to point out the early desert mothers as well as desert fathers: women her- mits, ascetics, and early monastics such as Apolinaria, Evgeniia, Evpraxiia, and Olimpiada. Citing women such as Blessed Aleksan- dra, who lived for ten years in a cave, Taisiia extols the strength, courage, and resolute character of these early ascetics. In a para- graph combining great pride in women's accomplishments with a formulaic reference to their weakness, she asserts:

> Women attained levels of asceticism equal to those of men, demonstrating amazing examples of self-denial and being blessed with great gifts from heaven. The heavenly fire, brought by the Sav- ior to earth, burned in the hearts of even these weaker creatures, women, and aroused in them a great flame of heavenly love which extinguished for them all earthly and temporal things, transforming them into nothingness.

Taisiia points out that women's monasticism, in the form of both the solitary life and the communal, developed at the same time as men's;

it constituted, in the words of St. John of Chrysostom, "a light, an embellishment, the glory and the crown of its perfection."[60] Taisiia counsels aspiring nuns that a life lived in imitation of these women would be a life well spent.

The letter on the responsibilities of choir sisters emphasizes the importance of performing one's duties intelligently, consciously and conscientiously. She is appalled at the thought of slipshod work in any form, quoting Jeremiah 48:10, "A curse on all who are slack in doing the Lord's work." It is clear that she identifies with the great importance of liturgical singing, believing that it can have a transformative effect on those listening. The choir is the mouth of the church, singing on behalf of the believers. It can change the spiritual disposition of those listening, awakening in their souls feelings of tenderness and repentance. And it can appeal to God for mercy on earthly sinners, which is "heavenly work—the work of angels, not of humans." For this reason it is essential to sing not only with one's lips and voice, but also with one's mind, soul, will, and desire—with all one's being.[61] She repeats several times the words of Psalm 47, "*poite razumno*," which means to sing with all one's intelligence, art, and skill.[62] And it is not surprising that this psalm should have great resonance for her, since it is filled with the spirit of the life-transforming dream she had as a student, a vision of God enthroned on high.

Throughout the book she stresses the higher responsibilities of those who have chosen the monastic life, including the responsibility of using one's gifts and talents in the service of God and the grave importance of not being a source of scandal to others. Painfully aware of the realities of convent life, she points to the pitfalls of communal life, including envy, idle gossip, and the difficulty of obedience. Interestingly, her chapter on mutual love never poses the question of "special friendships," the code word in monastic literature for excessive closeness and homosexual relationships.

Instead, perhaps based on her own experience, she starts from the assumption that others in the community might at times be a nuisance, a distraction to one's solitude and serenity. But the temptation to view one's neighbor this way must be fought against, for one cannot love God without loving one's neighbor. She quotes extensively from John, the "Apostle of Love," and from Paul's epistle to the Colossians: "Be forbearing with one another, and forgiving, where any of you has cause for complaint: you must forgive as the Lord forgave you. To crown all there must be love, to bind all together and to complete the whole" (Col 3:13–14). The whole was of paramount importance, for the monastic community was a family—a family united "in the one goal of the pleasing of God and the perfecting of self."[63]

In the chapter on prayer, she recounts the story told in her autobiography of Mother Feokfista and her remembrance of the old nun's enrapt prayer and expression of "angelic peace." She emphasizes that Feokfista was of simple peasant background, semiliterate or perhaps totally illiterate, and that her external life was one of ordinary, humble obediences; nonetheless, her inner life was extraordinary, one worthy of imitation by all. She gives several examples of contemporary models of holiness and prayerfulness, explaining to her readers:

> I deliberately gave you such [holy examples] from contemporary life because we, reading and hearing narratives of the great deeds of the saints, often say as an excuse "They were saints! . . . That happened in earlier times." That is why we must comprehend that even now there are true ascetics. Neither time nor place make a person holy, but one's own desire and firm will. Pray ardently and God will not fail in this blessing for you.[64]

Her final letter of instruction to beginning nuns is devoted to the ceremony of tonsuring, more commonly called in English "the taking of the veil." The rich symbolism of renunciation (the shorn hair), betrothal to Christ, and angelic transformation of the rite of tonsuring had moved both Margarita Tuchkova and Metropolitan Filaret to tears. In her chapter on tonsuring, Abbess Taisiia praises the monastic calling and the ceremony of tonsuring, exclaiming: "It is truly a great deed, the tonsuring into the holy angelic order. It is a great and mysterious power that is embodied in this sacred act, an act which holds up the angelic model, so that an individual can become like an angel in one's internal life." Angels are bodiless and the material world cannot become like them, but the inner world can. Nonetheless, she warns them that even after their tonsuring, they will be subject to many temptations. The walls of the cloister cannot keep out distracting and deceitful thoughts. Even while keeping vigil, they can be weighed down with earthly concerns; even while standing in prayer and psalmody, their thoughts can wander in all directions. When this happens, they must remember how blessed they are and how lofty it is to be the bride of Christ. If they keep this mental image before them, they will be able to "taste the Kingdom of God while still being on earth."[65] They can live in the two time zones, the present and the eternal.

It is clear from her letters of instruction to beginning nuns that Taisiia took most seriously her role as abbess and spiritual director of those entrusted to her. It was out of her sense of responsibility for their edification and ultimate salvation that her relationship with John of Kronstadt developed, a relationship that would last for nineteen years, until his death in 1908.

In the summer of 1891 Taisiia happened to be in the town of Cherepoutz, on the Volga river route, on monastery business. She learned that Father John of Kronstadt—who was renowned for his work with the working classes of Kronstadt and St. Petersburg, for the establishment of homes of industry for the poor, and for his stirring sermons and powerful prayers of intercession—was in Cherepoutz for the day. A local businessman had arranged for a large passenger ship to stop in Cherepoutz and take Father John along the route of his annual journey to his native village of Sura in Arkhangelsk province. Hearing of this, Taisiia immediately went to the house where John of Kronstadt was staying, forced her way through the large crowd that had gathered there, and insisted on meeting with him. When she did, she pleaded with him to come and visit her monastery, which was located on the shore of the river Sheksna. He excused himself from coming for fear that he would hold up the ship. She then descended on the owner of the ship, persuaded him to make a short stop at the monastery's dock, and dragooned Father John into visiting Leushino. When they had docked and were in a carriage on the way to the monastery, he turned to her and asked her, "Why did you ask me so vehemently to visit your monastery? We met and had a talk—isn't that enough?" She answered him, "Batiushka [father], I'm asking you to come because I had a chance to talk to you and see you with my own eyes. Having received this happiness, I want my sisters also to be as fortunate. If I don't use all means available to me to do this, then it will be on my conscience; but if I do everything on my part, and you still refuse, then I will not be answerable to God."[66]

During his short visit to the monastery, Father John was moved by everything he saw and had an intense soul-to-soul conversation with Taisiia about faith, prayer, and the worries and burdens of clerical positions of responsibility. When they parted, he promised to hold the monastery in his prayers and to visit it each summer on his way to Sura. He came to love these annual visits, especially delighting in the choral singing of the sisters and the beauty and serenity of the monastery. A ritual developed for his arrival. Taisiia would meet him at the dock and drive with him in the carriage for the two-mile ride to Leushino. As soon as they entered the large well-kept grounds of the monastery, he would begin to bless the land on both sides, saying, "Make it to grow, O Lord, and preserve all this for the use of the monastery where Thy Name is constantly glorified." As soon as they approached the monastery buildings, the sisters would greet them with loud, harmonious singing. They would continue singing while walking alongside the carriage up to the main church, where the clergy would meet them; there would be a joyful procession, and the celebration of the liturgy. Afterward, they would have tea in the garden, with Father John pouring for all from the samovar. They would also go out to the fields when the sisters were working there and have a large picnic for everyone, again accompanied by glorious singing.[67]

There were also moments of great solitude, of long walks in the woods, and of deep conversations between him and Abbess Taisiia. Taisiia cherished these conversations; noting his wisdom and spiritual perceptiveness, she told him, "You are a man endowed with grace; you see by the Holy Spirit which abides in you." Together they explored the inner soul, the feelings of the heart, as well as deeds and behavior. She confessed to him her feelings of depression, the times when she felt as if a black cloud were hanging over her head and there seemed to be no way past it. She also admitted to being a cautious, even distrustful person, afraid of the future and of being hurt by people; she attributed this feeling to the many times she had been hurt by people's dishonesty or injustice to her. To the problem of despondency, he told her that many had been destroyed by this spiritual temptation; if she would be "strong and manly" and carry this cross with endurance as a way of increasing her humility, then God would help her. To the second problem, suspicion and distrust of the future, he told her that she only hurt herself by imagining evil where there might be none. As long as she did evil to no one, she should not fear for the future.[68]

Abbess Taisiia and John of Kronstadt also engaged in long theological discussions, intellectual and spiritual exchanges that she particularly relished. One day when they were talking about faith, she expressed her view that faith is not as dark and blind as people say when they use the expression "blind faith." She believed that the mystery of faith is accessible to understanding, to the mind and even more so to the soul and the heart. As she explained, "It is not that I believe irresponsibly or blindly, but conscientiously, so to speak, groping in a sense for why, what reason, and how to believe." Reason and feeling together could help one comprehend the incomprehensible. Why even the great mystery of the Trinity, the Tri-hypostatic Divinity, could be explained, she said: "God the Father is the pre-eternal mind, God the Son is the pre-eternal word, God the Spirit is the life-giving, intellectual, hypostatic, all-powerful holiness, the life of lives." John of Kronstadt was somewhat taken aback by this, saying that it was given to very few to fathom such a mystery.[69] But Taisiia was passionately expressing what had been the work of a lifetime for her: the integration of intellect and intuition, of mind and heart, in experiencing and understanding the mysteries of the divine.

Besides the obvious virtues of piety, nonpossessiveness, and passionate love for God's cause, Taisiia was inspirational, inspiriting—literally enflaming in others—a spark of the divine spirit she experienced in her visions. She did this constantly, through her ordinary conversations with people, spiritual counseling, educational work, edificatory writings, and personal example. She also had a profound sense of the aesthetic, believing that the beauty of music, liturgical worship, church architecture, and nature itself could inspire the most humble peasant to lofty heights. In addition to her passion for liturgical music, she established an icon-painting workshop at Leushino, where the choir sisters and those gifted in art produced icons sold throughout the country. Cherishing Russia's architectural heritage, she was a fervid preservationist, restoring the ancient Ferapontov monastery with its famous icons and frescoes.[70] And the churches and various chapels she built at Leushino and in the other communities she founded brought the beauty of Orthodoxy into countless people's lives. It is not surprising that today in the former Soviet Union, the stunning onion-domed churches and monasteries of prerevolutionary Russia are being lovingly restored as a national cultural heritage, an antidote to the drabness of Stalinist and modern construction and a timeless memorial to humanity's seeking of the divine.

Taisiia also had her weaknesses and her waverings. She was highly sensitive to criticism, seeing slights where they might not have existed and sinking into deep distress, even paralysis, over slanders and calumnies. She wavered at times in her faith, sometimes overwhelmed by the tumultuousness of life. She once compared herself in a poem to the apostle Peter, who lacked sufficient faith to heed Christ's command to him during a storm to arise and walk on the sea:

The Sea of Life

Like Peter, I am sinking, falling
In waves of life's tumultuous sea;
As he did, so to Thee I'm calling:
"Oh Teacher, save me, rescue me!"

All-powerful! A single motion,
A word from Thee can calm the storm;
It's possible to tread the ocean,
The wind and thunder to transform.

Upon my heart's waves, I implore Thee,
With sacred feet do Thou now tread—
My heart will quiet down before Thee
And taste the peace Thou wilt shed.

> Stretch out Thy hand, my faith redouble,
> And, as to Peter, say: "O ye
> of little faith, what is thy trouble? . . .
> Take manly courage, come to Me!"[71]

As this poem indicates, Taisiia found encouragement and inspiration in a rich reservoir of saints and holy exemplars. We have seen how often she was empowered to undertake some daunting action by a dream or vision in which the Mother of God, a saint, or an angelic being inspired her to higher deeds and courageous acts. Her lexicon of inspiring figures was broad; though exclusively Christian, it was without boundaries of gender, place, or time. The desert mothers and fathers; various apostles; saints John the Baptist, Nicholas, Paraskeva, and Anthony of Kiev; the archangel Michael; and, of course, the Mother of God all presented themselves as supporters and exemplars with whom she could identify and on whom she could model herself. They were also powerful intercessors in the heavenly realm, whose prayers could bring grace on her and her community.

When Taisiia died in January 1915, she had been abbess of Leushino convent for thirty years, had helped to found six other women's religious communities, had been awarded two pectoral crosses, one from the Holy Synod in 1889 and one from Emperor Alexander III in 1892. She had also been personally presented gifts for her educational work from Emperor Nicholas II and Empress Alexandra in 1910, 1911, and 1913.[72] The journal of the Novgorod diocese published shortly after her death a stirring memorial to her, declaring her one of Russia's most famous nuns, a woman "renowned for her piety, education and Christian enlightenment, to which were connected the rare gifts of administration and enterprise."[73] At her burial, Father Alexander Svetlovsky, a priest of the Leushino convent, delivered a sermon summing up her goals and accomplishments:

From the very first steps of her activity the late Abbess had as her aim not only to confirm piety amidst the sisters, but also to draw people close to the Church, to give them the possibility of seeing and enjoying the beauty of the services of our Orthodox Church, to provide fulfillment of their religious needs. For this purpose she built temples. All her life, until her last minute, she actively participated in taking care of them. Concern for the Church did not abandon her even on her death-bed. Simultaneously, she wanted and was striving for the church-oriented way of life, planted in her monastery, to progress even beyond the life of the monastery, to enter and penetrate into all the pores, so to speak, of the daily life of the peasants. With this aim, she founded a one-classroom school at first, then a two-classroom school, and finally even a teachers' school which exists to this day. You know from experience how hard it is here, amidst the moss and swamps, to create and maintain even a small school, and how even more difficult it is to create a higher educational center, and yet more a teachers' school. But what can love not accomplish? And in truth the love of the deceased for this holy task succeeded in accomplishing it all."[74]

Archimandrite Antonii, who served the memorial *panakhida* (prayer service for the dead), expressed assurance that the virtues that so distinguished her—faith, fervent love, and nonacquisitiveness—would comprise, so to speak, a bouquet of flowers she could present without fear to the King of Heaven.[75]

We know what virtues Taisiia had aspired to from her autobiography, a rare thing for a woman to write, even rarer for a nun. To write an autobiography is to draw attention to the significance of one's own experience, and such an undertaking had to be justified. Not surprisingly, Taisiia begins her autobiography with a clear disclaimer:

> It is not by my own wish or volition that I am beginning to write these notes; not only is it not according to my wish, but it is even against it. I am doing it only in obedience to people incomparably more experienced, more intelligent and more spiritually-minded than

I—people known not only to me, the wretched one, but to all those who are zealous to lead a God-pleasing life and to save their souls.[76]

The first one to urge her to write down her visions was Abbot Feodosii, who heard her confession during her pilgrimage to the Monastery of the Caves in 1885. Having been long troubled that her apparitions might be just delusions from the enemy, she described them at length to Feodosii and asked for his discernment. Not finding anything dangerous in them, he saw them as signs of God's mercy to Taisiia and advised her strongly to put them down in writing, not only for herself but also for the benefit of others. She hesitated for several years to do this, thinking, "Who am I, that through me, a sinner, the Lord might benefit those who are much worthier than I?" It was only when Father John of Kronstadt insisted that she put in writing all the spiritual visions given to her, which he believed had great significance, that she undertook her spiritual autobiography. There were times when it seemed impossible to her to put into human words "that which cannot be explained, which comes from on high." When overwhelmed by the audacity and the difficulty of this undertaking, she found comfort in the words of St. Paul, that God's grace and "strength is made perfect in weakness." (2 Cor 12:9).[77]

The reticence to write about oneself, to give one's own life the significance and coherence that autobiography demands, is not peculiar to religious women in whom the pull toward humility might seem most acute. In *Writing a Woman's Life*, a critical study of women's biographies and autobiographies, Carolyn Heilbrun notes that until recently women have written few autobiographies and when they have, they have rarely told the truth about their lives. They tend to play down their accomplishments, mute their seeking of power and control, and be silent about their anger and pain.[78] Accomplishment and achievement have been internalized as inexcusable in a female

self; only those who have been called by God or Christ or who have
had some other higher calling, whether Florence Nightingale,
Dorothy Day, or Emma Goldman, might begin to speak of their accomplishments, and even then, ambivalently.[79] Taisiia's autobiography fits largely within the genre of the high spiritual autobiography,
but it also contains qualities of the honest autobiography Heilbrun
pleads for from women. Her natural abilities are attributed to God, as
are most of her accomplishments, but she is clearly proud of them.
She is honest about her anger about losing her favorite cell and having to obey those whose judgment she could not respect. Her struggles with her mother are clearly laid out, as is her fear of being
swallowed up in family responsibilities. The pain of being herself and
following her own path is also movingly expressed: the pain of being
gifted and of trying to follow a higher path while slogging around in
the ordinary mud of life, with its jealousies and depressions.

Taisiia accepted as universal the Christian call to humility but
tried to inculcate into the young, predominantly peasant women
she trained a sense of pride in their lofty calling to be the brides of
Christ and a constant sense of responsibility for their own actions.
By writing of her own spiritual experience, she was also asserting
the equal authority of women's experience, an important claim and
a perspective sorely needed for the fullest understanding of God's
ways of working in this world.[80]

Feminist theologians have articulated the pain many modern
women experience in the dominantly male symbols of Godhead,
sainthood, and priesthood.[81] Taisiia's writings give us no expression
of this pain. As we have noted, she not only drew inspiration from
but also identified with a wide range of male and female saints as
well as genderless angels. Even her imaging of God seems remark-
ably inclusive. In the introduction to her autobiography, she recalls
the feeling of well-being she has had throughout her life, because
God has been with her: "All my life long the Lord has been seeking

me, the sinner, and guided me by His right hand, like a mother guides an unreasonable child, to prevent it, unable to walk along slippery paths, from falling and injuring itself."[82] God as father and God as mother both protected her on life's journey.

Throughout that journey, Taisiia's eyes, mind, and soul were lifted upward, even while she might be checking on the number of bricks delivered to the convent for a stone wall or the quality of soup being served in the refectory. Her dominant metaphor was of a God on high, but she also wrote frequently of the God within and the sweetness of that feeling. She lived in the high hopes of heaven, and of experiencing the heavenly while on earth.

In many Orthodox churches, Abbess Taisiia is honored on January 2, the day of her repose. The appointed vespers reading for that day promises a heavenly reward for the just, a reward for which she ardently hoped. It is a fitting commemorative to Taisiia's deepest beliefs: "But the just live forever; their reward is in the Lord's keeping, and the Most High has them in his care" (Wis 5:15)[83]

♦

Conclusion

oday the term *holiness* seems old-fashioned; we are more comfortable speaking of spirituality. History shows that the perception and labeling of goodness change with time and place. In this sense, holiness is socially constructed and requires cultural support.

The women we have studied were considered holy in their day. Their gutsy refusals to lead a conventional life and their determination to undertake instead the rigors of ascetic fasting, of living alone or living in the company of women, of foregoing a visit to a dying mother because of belief in a higher calling, and of disposing of property to follow their own inner authority—all could be sanctioned by the religious culture of nineteenth-century Russia. In another culture these women might have been called witches, or bitches, or anorexics.[1] In the atheistic world of twentieth-century Communist Russia, they were branded as parasites, obscurantists, and class enemies. Women and men like them were imprisoned by the thousands as a new government, with a new belief in a higher cause, tried to impose its own set of moral and ethical beliefs. Between 1921 and 1923, 2,691 married priests, 1,962 monks, 3,447 nuns, and numerous laity were killed.[2] Churches, monasteries, and the communities founded by women like Margarita Tuchkova and Matrona Popova were ruthlessly suppressed, despite the protests of the local population.[3]

Marxists argued that religion was a false consciousness, an opiate that blinded the poor to their own oppression. Believing that religion created an illusory sense of unity among people by blurring class lines, they urged the oppressed to overthrow religion and unite in class solidarity.

The women we have studied believed deeply that they were united with each other and with all of humanity through the parenthood of God. As earthly children of a heavenly God, they shared an ontological equality, a radical sisterhood and brotherhood, that cut across class divides, rendering rich and poor, male and female, one in their shared humanity. They believed that all human beings had been created one in God's eyes—they were one before their fall into sin, and they were one in Christ's salvific vision. St. Paul argued that in the radically redeemed world of Christ, "there is neither slave nor free, neither male nor female" (Gal 3:28). And in this world of the here and now, all human beings were one in the deepest experiences of their life—in their grief, their joy, their suffering, their longing for love. Margarita Tuchkova's holiness was, for example, rooted in this belief. Her profound sensitivity to those in grief and mourning and her loving response to them came from a shared human experience of loss, an experience that rendered class and social standing irrelevant.

And yet class and gender differences were far from irrelevant in the lives of the women we have studied. Women of noble origin, like Margarita, Angelina, and Taisiia, had advantages of wealth and education, which were evident in their relative control and disposal of property, in their managerial skills, and in their belief in their varied obligations to raise the poor and the uneducated to a higher level of life. Taisiia revealed herself as condescending on occasion to the ignorant peasant girls entering the community, and Margarita admitted to using perfume to anesthetize herself to the most offensive smells of poverty and homelessness. As for the peasant women,

Anastasiia's inability to own property prevented her from founding the community she dreamed of at Kurikha, and Matrona's holiness partly unfolded in her assumption of the class-transgressing virtues of munificence and beneficence.

Gender realities revealed themselves in the greater emphasis for women than for men on family responsibilities, including the care of parents, and the greater admonition to them to wait on God. Anastasiia postponed for over twenty years her heartfelt desire to live as a hermit while caring for her elderly parents. Margarita and Angelina came into control of their property and their lives only as widows. Despite a clear, early calling on Angelina's part to a more contemplative life and the building of a sacred church, she could only fulfill these wishes after the death of her husband, a husband who had been picked for her at the age of fifteen. Social strictures placed greater constraints on women's life choices than on men's and meant that the turning to a dedicated religious life often had a life-cycle aspect for women: they were more able to fulfill their spiritual desires in mid-life, after taking care of responsibilities to husbands, parents, and children. In this, the experience of Anastasiia, Angelina, and Margarita partly supports recent scholarship on medieval and early modern European saints that suggests that both the life patterns and the forms of piety of holy women differed from those of men. Donald Weinstein and Rudolph Bell have argued that male saints were more likely to undergo abrupt adolescent conversions, involving renunciation of wealth, power, marriage, and sexuality, whereas women's lives were characterized by earlier vocations, greater continuity, and less dramatic actions.[4] Caroline Bynum has argued that it is because women lacked control over their wealth and marital status that "their life stories show fewer heroic gestures of casting aside money, property and family"; instead, women more often used their ordinary experiences—of powerlessness, of service, of nurturing, and of sickness—"as symbols into which they poured ever deeper and more paradoxical meanings."[5] The experience of these Russian women confirms that women had less control over their lives and property than men but suggests a life-cycle aspect, demonstrating that women like Anastasiia and Angelina could pursue in mid-life what they had dreamed of in adolescence or early adulthood.

At the same time, there were women like Taisiia and Matrona, as well as countless numbers of *chernichki, spasennnitsy,* religious sisters, novices, and nuns who chose and effected a spiritually motivated celibate life as young women. They were able, albeit with difficulty, to overthrow the socially prescribed roles of wife and mother because the religious beliefs of their culture contained both affirmation of social conventions and the seeds of the subversion of those conventions for a higher life. It is one of the paradoxes of established religions that they begin in radicalism, become in time enmeshed in the social hierarchies of their culture, but always contain at their core a set of values at variance with the values of the world. Religion, by its very nature, privileges the eternal over the temporal. People of deep religious faith, whether living in a society constrained by the arrogance of the medieval church, the greed of capitalism, or the ruthlessness of communism, can uphold and experience an alternate vision—the loving and liberating freedom of the divine.

Experiences of the divine sustained and empowered the women of this book. Disposed to see everywhere the presence of God, they found it in abundant measure. In their eyes, the world was filled with love, a love that called for response. The someone or something calling them to love they named God, and they structured their lives to be open to this call. They believed that in the contemplative life, they could heighten those qualities of spirit revered by Orthodoxy—a receptivity and openness to God and his creation. Moments in which they felt alive with the presence of God constituted the joy and the meaning of their lives.

Such contemplative moments are not the preserve of monastics or even of the consciously religious. As Gerald May has recently argued in *The Awakened Heart*, a study of contemplative psychology:

> Contemplation happens to everyone. It happens in moments when we are open, undefended, and immediately present. People who are called contemplatives are simply those who seek the expansion of the moments, who desire to live in that quality of presence more fully and continually.[6]

Contemplation is a psychological state, a way of apprehending the world. It combines a clarity of perception with a willing receptivity to that which is—an acute experience and acceptance of things as they are. A contemplative moment is a moment of sheer openness—the moment before we are conscious of our response. Contemplation is, thus, a natural response, as natural as being seared by the beauty of autumn leaves. But some people, including many artists and mystics, consciously nurture the natural gift of contemplation, developing an intentionality about it; those people who direct their intentionality toward love transform natural contemplation into spiritual contemplation.[7]

Spiritual contemplation is aimed toward love and arises from love. For the women of this book, this love was God. They gave thanks for the graced moments when they felt the immediacy of its presence and simplified and disciplined their lives to heighten their receptivity to its beauty and pain. Wishing to linger in these moments of communion with God, they found themselves slowly transforming their lives to remove the interfering clutter, chatter, and phoniness. In describing the transformative aspects of spiritual life, Evelyn Underhill notes that "all the responses of men to the incitement of this hidden God . . . follow much the same road": on the one hand, "renunciation of the narrow horizon, the personal ambition, the unreal objective" and, on the other hand, "a deliberate and grateful response to the attraction of the unseen." Traditional spiritual writers have called these two activities mortification and prayer, formidable words for modern men and women. Yet, as Underhill explains, they only mean, when translated into our own language, that the development of the spiritual life involves both dealing with ourselves and attending to the divine. Above all, they mean:

> first turning to Reality, and then getting our tangled, half-real psychic lives . . . into harmony with the great movement of Reality. Mortification means killing the very roots of self-love, pride and possessiveness, anger and violence, ambition and greed in all their disguises, however respectable these disguises may be. . . . In fact, it really means the entire transformation of our personal, professional and political life into something more consistent with our real situation as small, dependent, fugitive creatures; all sharing the same limitations and inheriting the same half-animal past.[8]

This may not sound very impressive or unusual, but it is the foundation of all spiritual life, not simply of Christianity. Indeed, as Underhill observes, "Wherever we find people whose spiritual life is robust and creative, we find that in one way or another this transformation has been effected and this price has been paid."[9]

The practices of mortification and prayer are practices of cleansing and communion. Together they help effect an interior personal transformation from the solipsistic bubble of our phony and anxious selves to a true, trusting inner self. This authentic self, liberated from sham and posturing, is capable of real, loving encounters with others and with God.

The goal of the monastic life is the transformation of self, from ego, anxiety, and alienation to compassion, freedom, and union. The women of this book, wishing to throw off the weight of human sin and deception for the lightness of divine transparency, often visualized the path of transformation as an angelic one. Anastasiia, in her stunning translucence, represented most clearly this holy emptying of self, but all of these women radiated, at least in visionary moments, a joyful serenity and simplicity.

In many ways, their virtues were quite traditional: faith, piety, chastity, compassion, and charity. Matrona, Anastasiia, and Angelina seem to have had a gladness of heart about them, whereas Margarita always bore a mark of sadness, and Taisiia, of struggle. Situating themselves within a specific tradition of Orthodox contemplative spirituality and modeling themselves after ancient saints and holy exemplars, they nonetheless each had a creative freshness to their spiritual life. Although they adhered to a common norm, each followed her own private prayer practice and had her own favorite *akathist*, psalm, saint, place of pilgrimage, and spiritual director. The particular form varied in which each woman most distinctively expressed her love of neighbor, with the ministry to others rooted in her deepest pain and despair. This experience of pain and redemption infused each one's holiness, giving it an embodied, compelling freshness. Out of her own wounding loss of husband and son, Margarita reached out to grieving widows and mothers; out of the loneliness of her orphaned childhood, Matrona touched the homeless, the orphaned, and the strays of society. Anastasiia gathered disciples to her as Melaniia, sensing her starvation for spiritual nourishment, had once gathered her. Angelina, who had long yearned for a contemplative life, offered it abundantly to poor peasant women. Taisiia, taunted as a child for her intellectual gifts and spiritual sensitivity, devoted herself to the education of young women and nuns and struggled throughout her life to interweave a critical intellect with a deep faith.

Community was an essential part of their spirituality. Living and worshipping with each other, they helped to create, shape, and expand a new form of women's religious community, the *zhenskaia obshchina*. Unlike the idiorhythmic monasteries that formed a strong part of the Orthodox tradition, women's religious communities were communal in nature; economically and structurally, they were usually agricultural communities with an egalitarian emphasis on communal labor. Unlike the state-supported *shtatnye* monasteries with their limited budgets and high entrance donations, women's religious communities, through their collaborative, self-supporting agricultural structure, were able to offer poor women a means of undertaking a dedicated religious life. In an environment supportive of a turning to the divine, a community of like-minded women, though of varying social background, could reconcile the gap between the high culture of the educated elite and the popular culture of the peasantry. Thus, early in the century, a noble woman such as Margarita can be found reading scriptural and patristic readings in the evenings to the simple women gathered around her, while, later in the century, Angelina and Taisiia pattern communities that encouraged literacy, education, and the dignity belonging to brides of Christ. Women's religious communities, with their greater emphasis on charitable activity, infused traditional Orthodox monasticism with a more active, social quality. The monastic culture they shaped embraced those qualities of goodness—communitarianism, pluralism, and relationalism—that the feminist theologian Anne Carr has suggested would mark soteriology (the doctrine of salvation through Christ) if women wrote their own theology.[10]

Finally, integration was an important goal of the holy life. In providing a meeting ground for and a link between the various classes, women's religious communities of the nineteenth and early twentieth centuries actualized a hoped-for reintegration of a fractured Russian society. Similarly, personal integration—a wholeness of being—was viewed as a mark of the transformed, god-imitating individual. Religious models of personal transformation supported men in claiming qualities of self traditionally associated with the feminine, such as humility and compassion, while allowing women to assert determination, authority, and responsibility, qualities usually associated with the masculine.

It is difficult for many feminists to believe that patriarchal religious traditions can empower women. And it is difficult for modern readers, in general, to accept that tradition can be a path of creativity and a source of liberation. Yet the experience of the women of this book argues that the established disciplines of monastic tradition—routines of prayer, meditation, contemplative silence, fasting, and mortification—can be powerful tools for breaking through human mire and suffering to a transcendent freedom. Because holiness goes beyond false attachments and splintered selves to the inner core of being, it allows both women and men to be fully whole and powerful, radiating a life force and fresh energy stunning to its observers.

It is my hope that the recovered memory of these holy women and their contemplative tradition will help Russia—and us—reclaim a vital spiritual energy and a rich creativity.

◆

Notes

Introduction

1. See Brenda Meehan-Waters, "Popular Piety, Local Initiative and the Founding of Women's Religious Communities in Russia, 1764–1917," in *St. Vladimir's Theological Quarterly*, 25 (1986): 117–42, and idem., "Metropolitan Filaret (Drozdov) and the Reform of Russian Women's Monastic Communities," in *Russian Review*, 50 (1991): 310–23.
2. *The Orthodox Word*, no. 133 (1987): 69.
3. John A. Coleman, "Conclusion: After Sainthood?" in John Stratton Hawley, ed. *Saints and Virtues* (Berkeley: Univ. of California Press, 1987), 209.
4. Peter Brown, "The Saint as Exemplar in Late Antiquity," in Hawley, ed. *Saints and Virtues*, 12.
5. For a discussion of the loss in modern secular cultures of the ability to perceive sanctity, see Coleman, "Conclusion," 205–08.
6. Nicholas Arseniev, *Russian Piety* (New York: St. Vladimir's Press, 1964), 34–35, 75–76.
7. *Little Russian Philokalia*, vol. 1, St. Seraphim of Sarov (Platina, CA: St. Herman of Alaska Brotherhood, 1980), 53.
8. Taisiia, Ig. *Pis'ma k novonachal'noi inokine o glavneishikh obiazannostiakh inocheskoi zhizni. Sostavleno na osnovanii sviatootecheskikh asketicheskikh Pisanii, prierov Sv. Ottsev i mnogoletnogo sobstvennogo opyta* (St. Petersburg, 1909), 8.
9. J. H. Newman, *The Church of the Fathers* (1840), quoted in A. M. Allchin, *The Silent Rebellion. Anglican Religious Communities, 1845–1900* (London: SCM Press, 1958), 56.
10. Quoted in Kenneth Leech, *Soul Friend. The Practice of Christian Spirituality* (San Francisco: Harper & Row, 1980), 45.
11. Leech, "Soul Friend," vii.
12. Richard J. Foster, *Celebration of Discipline. The Path to Spiritual Growth*, rev. exp. ed. (San Francisco: Harper & Row, 1988); Tilden Edwards, *Living Simply Through the Day. Spiritual Survival in a Complex Age* (New York: Paulist Press,

◆ Notes ◆

1977); Evelyn Underhill, *The Spiritual Life* (Harrisburg: Morehouse Publishing, 1955); and Bruce Davis, *Monastery Without Walls. Daily Life in the Silence* (Berkeley, CA: Celestial Arts, 1990).

13. For a discussion of relational psychology and the feminist distinction between living *for* others and *with* others, see Carter Heyward, *Touching Our Strength: The Erotic as Power and the Love of God* (San Francisco: Harper San Francisco, 1989), 14.

A Historical Note

1. James Cracraft, *The Church Reform of Peter the Great* (London: Macmillan, 1971).

2. *Polnoe sobranie postanovlenii i rasporiazhenii po vedomstvu pravoslavnogo ispovedaniia.* (Hereafter *PSPR*). *Tsarstvovanie imperatritsy Ekateriny Alekseevny*, no. 167 (28 February 1764).

3. V. V. Zverinskii, *Material dlia istoriko-topograficheskogo issledovaniia o pravoslavnykh monastyriakh v rossiiskoi imperii*, vol. 1 (St. Petersburg, 1890), xi.

4. *Idiorhythmic* is a term used in the Eastern Orthodox church to describe monasteries in which the monks live separately; hold property; work individually in supporting themselves; and, though members of a monastery supervised by an elected council, are not under daily direct supervision.

5. Marie Thomas, "Muscovite Convents in the 17th Century," *Russian History*, pt. 2 (1983): 234–35; Sophia Senyk, *Women's Monasteries in Ukraine and Belorussia to the Period of Suppressions*, vol. 222, *Orientalia Christiana Analecta* (Rome, 1983), 154–64; I. F. Tokmakov, *Istoricheskoe opisanie moskovskogo novodevich'iago monastyria* (Moscow, 1885), 119–20.

6. This is my figure compiled from data in L. I. Denisov, *Pravoslavnye monastyri rossiiskoi imperii. Polnyi spisok vsekh 1105 nyne sushchestvuiushchikh v 75 guberniakh oblastiakh Rossii i 2 inostrannykh gosudarstvakh muzhskikh, zhenskikh monastyrei, arkhiereiskikh domov i zhenskikh obshchin* (Moscow, 1908) and V. Zverinskii, 2 vols. (St. Petersburg, 1890), and in the archives of the Holy Synod in St. Petersburg.

7. Claire Louise Claus, "Die Russischen Frauenklöster um die Wende des 18. Jahrhunderts, Ihre Karitative Tätigkeit und Religiöse Bedeutung," *Kirche im Osten* (Amsterdam, 1969), band 4 (1961): 147.

8. A. G. Rashin, *Naselenie Rossii za 100 let* (Moscow, 1956), 284; Rose Glickman, *Russian Factory Women. Workplace and Society, 1880–1914* (Berkeley: Univ. of California Press, 1984), 16.

9. *Bol' shaia sovetskaia entsiklopediia*, 3rd. ed., vol. 22 (Moscow, 1975), 246; *The Great Soviet Encyclopedia. A Translation of the Third Edition*, vol. 22 (New York: Macmillan, 1979), 424.

10. For statistical tables on the literacy of the Tvorozhkovo community, see Brenda Meehan-Waters, "To Save Oneself: Russian Peasant Women and the

154

Development of Women's Religious Communities in Prerevolutionary Russia," in Beatrice Farnsworth and Lynne Viola, eds. *Russian Peasant Women* (New York: Oxford Univ. Press, 1992), 128–29.

11. This is my compilation based on data from Synod archives: Rossiiskii gosudarstvennyi istoricheskii arkhiv (hereafter RGIA), f. 797 (Chancellery of the Over-Procuror of the Holy Synod), op. 33, II-3, d. 207, "So svedeniami o vsekh, nakhodiavshikhsia v imperii monastyriakh, obshchinakh i pustyniakh, 29 ianv.–20 okt. 1903 (Nizhegorod, ll. 2-5, Tambov, ll. 18-18 ob., Novgorod, ll. 94 ob.-97, Moscow, ll. 206 ob.-256).

Chapter One: Margarita Tuchkova

1. T. Tolycheva (E. V. Novosil'tseva), *Spaso-Borodinskii monastyr' i ego osnovatel'nitsa. Posviashchaetsia vsem pochitaiushchim pamiat' Margarity Mikhailovny Tuchkovoi*, 3rd. ed. (Moscow, 1889), 4–5. According to internal evidence, Tolycheva's book was written in 1874, twenty-two years after Tuchkova's death; she spoke with many people, both members of the community and neighboring peasants, who had known Tuchkova and shared their memories of her.
2. Ibid.
3. Ibid., 7.
4. Ibid., 8.
5. *The New Encyclopedia Britannica. Micropaedia*, vol. 2 (Chicago and London: Encyclopedia Britannica, 1978), 171.
6. Tolycheva, 14.
7. Taisiia, comp., *Russkoe pravoslavnoe zhenskoe monashestvo XVIII-XX v.* (Hereafter *RPZhM*.) (Jordanville: Holy Trinity Monastery, 1985), 38.
8. Letter of 6 April 1817. Tolycheva, 20–21.
9. Tolycheva, 17–18.
10. Ibid., 19–21.
11. Ibid., 18.
12. Ibid., 19.
13. *RPZhM*, 38.
14. Tolycheva, 23.
15. *The New English Bible with the Apocrypha. Oxford Study Edition* (New York: Oxford University Press, 1976), 735.
16. Tolycheva, 24.
17. *RPZhM*, 38.
18. Tolycheva, 26.
19. Ibid., 28.
20. Ibid.
21. Ibid, 28–29.
22. Filaret (Drozdov), Pis'ma moskovskogo mitropolita Filareta k igumenii spaso-borodinskogo monastyria Sergii, ed. Savva, arkhiepiskop tverskii i kashinskii (Tver, 1890), iii.

◆ *Notes* ◆

23. Tolycheva, 30. Archbisop Savva, who edited Filaret's letter's to Abbess Sergia, Tuchkova's successor, gives the figure for 1833 of fifty-three, including "hermits and workers." (*Pis'ma. . . Filareta k. . . Sergii*, iii.)
24. Tolycheva, 28–30.
25. For a general discussion of church-state relations under Nicholas I, see David W. Edwards, "The System of Nicholas I in Church-State Relations," in Robert L. Nichols and Theofanis Stavrou, eds. *Russian Orthodoxy Under the Old Regime* (Minneapolis: Univ. of Minnesota, 1978), 154–69.
26. Tuchkova manumitted her serfs to the legal category of *vol'nye khlebopashtsy.*
27. Tolycheva, 30–31.
28. *RPZhM*, 40.
29. Tolycheva, 33.
30. For a list of the benefactors, see Tolycheva, 32.
31. *RPZhM*, 39–40.
32. Tolycheva, 32.
33. Letter printed in Tolycheva, 48–49.
34. *RPZhM*, 40; Tolycheva, 49. On the order of deaconess in the early Christian church, see JoAnn McNamara, *A New Song: Celibate Women in the First Three Christian Centuries* (New York: Haworth Press, 1983), 60–62; on the order of deaconess in the contemporary Orthodox church, see *Orthodox Women. Their Role and Participation in the Orthodox Church* (Geneva: World Council of Churches, 1977), 37–43, 49–50. See also Brenda Meehan-Waters, "From Contemplative Practice to Charitable Activity: Russian Women's Religious Communities and the Development of Charitable Work," in Kathleen McCarthy, ed. *Lady Bountiful Revisited: Women, Philanthropy, and Power* (New Brunswick: Rutgers Univ. Press, 1990).
35. RGIA, f. 797, op. 18, d. 41533, " Po otnosh. Dezhur. Gener. Glav. Sht. ego Min. Velich. o dostavleniiu svedenii kasatel'no sposobov soderzhaniia Spaso-Borodinskogo zhenskogo mon. i o predostavlenii v pol'zu onago na vechnyi vremena poluchaemogo igumenieiu Mariieiu (Tuchkovoiu) pensiona, 11 mar. 1848—3 okt. 1852, ll. 3-3 ob.
36. Tolycheva, 32.
37. Filaret, *Pis'ma . . . Filareta . . . k Sergii*, 3–7.
38. Quoted in Tolycheva, 34.
39. Quoted in Tolycheva, 38.
40. Letter quoted in Tolycheva, 37–38.
41. Quoted in Tolycheva, 34.
42. In his introduction to Filaret's letters to Abbess Sergiia, Savva speaks of "hermits and workers" in the early Borodino colony (*Pis'ma . . . Filareta . . . k Sergii*, iii).
43. Tolycheva, 33.
44. *Mneniia, otzyvy i pis'ma Filareta, mitropolita moskovskogo i kolomenskogo po raznym voprosam za 1821–1867gg.*, ed. L. Brodskii (Moscow, 1905), 167.

◆ Notes ◆

45. Filaret, *Pis'ma mitropolita moskovskogo Filareta k namestniku sviatotroitskiia sergievy lavry arkhimandritu Antoniiu, 1831–1867 gg.*, vol. 3 (Moscow, 1877–84), 165–66.
46. Filaret, *Pis'ma . . . Filareta k Sergii*, 45.
47. RGIA, f. 797, op. 18, d. 41553, l. 1-1 ob.; Filaret, *Mneniia*, 164–66.
48. Tolycheva, 46.
49. Tolycheva, 47–48.
50. Tolycheva, 50–51.
51. Tolycheva quotes peasants referring to Tuchkova as *sviataia* and our "true mother" (*rodnaia mat'*), Tolycheva, 3.
52. Tolycheva, 63. The quotations are from the King James version of the Bible.
53. *RPZhM*, 40.
54. Filaret, *Pis'ma . . . filareta k Sergii*, 12.
55. Denisov, 518; Pimen, "Vospominaniia arkhimandrita Pimena, nastoiatelia Nikolaevskogo monastyria, chto na Ugreshe," *Chteniia v Imperatorskom Obshchestve istorii i drevnostei rossiiskikh pri moskovskom universitete*, 1877, kn.1: 288–92; Brenda Meehan-Waters, "The Authority of Holiness: Women Ascetics and Spiritual Elders in Nineteenth-Century Russia," in Geoffrey A. Hosking, ed. *Church, Nation and State in Russia and Ukraine* (London: Macmillan, 1991), pp. 43–47.
56. Pimen, 300–303.
57. Meehan-Waters, "Popular Piety," 130–35.
58. Denisov, 522.
59. Tsentralnyi gosudarstvennyi istoricheskii arkhiv goroda Moskvy (hereafter TsGIAg Moskvy), f. 203 (Moskovskaia dukhovnaia konsistoriia), op. 763, d. 119, "Posluzhnye spiski nastoiatel'nitsy, monakhin i poslushnits Spaso-Borodinskogo monastyria i vedomost' of umershikh monakhiniakh i poslushnits etogo monastyria," 12 noiabr. 1914 g., ll. 3 ob.-20.

Chapter Two: Anastasiia Logacheva

1. Aleksandr Priklonskii, *Zhizn' pustynnitsy Anastasii Semenovny Logachevoi, vposledstvii monakhinia Afanasii, i voznikovenia na meste eia podvigov zhenskoi obshchiny* (Moscow, 1902), 3–5. An English translation exists under the title *Blessed Athanasia. Disciple of St. Seraphim*, by Fr. Alexander Priklonsky (Platina, CA: St. Herman of Alaska Brotherhood, 1980).
2. *Little Russian Philokalia*, vol. 1, *St. Seraphim* (Platina, CA: St. Herman of Alaska Brotherhood, 1978), 59.
3. Ibid., 23.
4. Sergius Bolshakoff, *Russian Mystics* (Kalamazoo, MI: Cistercian Publications, 1976), 253.
5. Priklonskii, 5–6.

157

6. Compare the lives of holy men and women in the twelve-volume *Zhizneopisaniia otechestvennykh podvizhnikov blagochestiia 18 i 19 vekov*, 12 vols. (Moscow, 1906–10).

7. N. Dobrotvotrskii, "Krest'ianskie iuridicheskie obychai: Po materialam, sobrannym v vostochnoi chasti Vladimirskoi gubernii (*uezdy* Viaznikovskii, Gorokhovetskii, Shuiskii i Kovrovskii). *Iuridicheskii vestnik*, May 1889, 270. On *chernichki* see L. A. Tul'tseva, "Chernichki," *Nauka i religiia*, 11 (1970): 80–82, and M. M. Gromyko, *Traditsionnye normy povedeniia i formy obshcheniia russkikh krest'ian XIX v.* (Moscow, 1986), 103–5.

8. S. V. Bulgakoff, comp. *Nastol'naia kniga dlia sviashchenno-tserkovno-sluzhitelei. Sbornik svedenii, kasaiushchikhsia preimuchchestvenno prakticheskoi deiatel'nosti otchestvennogo dukhovenstvo*, 2nd ed. (Khar'kov, 1900), 1201.

9. Priklonskii, 12.

10. Ibid., 11.

11. Ibid., 16.

12. Susan Ashbrook Harvey, *Asceticism and Society in Crisis. John of Ephesus and the Lives of the Eastern Saints* (Berkeley: Univ. of California Press, 1990), 6–7.

13. Dana Greene, *Evelyn Underhill. Artist of the Infinite Life* (New York: Crossroad, 1990), 6–7.

14. Priklonskii, 11.

15. "Pustynitsa Anastasiia Semenova Logacheva, vposledstvii monakhinia Afanasiia," *Zhizneopisaniia otechestvennykh podvizhnikov blagochestiia 18 i 19 vekom*, 2 (Moscow, 1907), 183.

16. For the phrase "jarring translucence" in relation to the ascetic, see Sebastian P. Brock and Susan Ashbrook Harvey, *Holy Women of the Syrian Orient* (Berkeley: Univ. of California Press, 1987), 12.

17. Priklonskii, 12.

18. Ibid., 16–18.

19. Greene, *Evelyn Underhill*, 5.

20. Priklonskii, 19.

21. Donald Weinstein and Rudolph M. Bell, *Saints and Society: The Two Worlds of Western Christendom, 1000–1700* (Chicago: Univ. of Chicago Press, 1982), 154.

22. Priklonskii, 20–21.

23. Ibid., 21–22.

24. Ibid., 22–25.

25. Ibid., 26.

26. Ibid., 25–26.

27. RGIA, f. 796, op. 144, d. 135, "Po khodataistvu barnaul'skogo 3 gil'dii kuptsa Afanasiia ob uchrezhdenii v Altaiiskikh gorakh, Tomskoi gub., zhenskoi obshchiny," 23 Ianv. 1863–19 Dek. 1864, ll. 9-18. On the missionary activity of the Russian Orthodox Church, see David M. Collins, "The Role of the Orthodox Missionary in the Altai: Archimandrite Makarii and V. I. Verbitskii," in Geoffrey A. Hosking, ed. *Church, Nation and State*, 96–107, and S. A. Smirnov,

"Missionerskaia deiate'nost' tserkvi (Vtoraia polovina XIXV.-1917 G.)," in A. I. Klibanov, ed. *Russkoe pravoslavie: vekhi istorii* (Moscow, 1989), 438–62.

28. Ibid., 11. 17-18 ob.

29. "Pamiati pustynnozhitel'nitsy Anastasii Semenovny Logachevoi (inokini Afanasii), *Zhizneopisaniia. Dopolnenie*, pt. 2 (Moscow, 1916), 256.

30. Ibid., 259.

31. Denisov, 550.

32. *Service Book of the Holy Orthodox-Catholic Apostolic Church,* comp., trans., and arranged from the Old Church-Slavonic Service Books of the Russian Church and Collated with the Service Books of the Greek Church, by Isabel Florence Hapgood, 3rd ed. (New York: Syrian Antiochian Orthodox Archdiocese of New York and All North America, 1956), 19. According to the Russian Orthodox Psalter, this is Psalm 62.

33. Peter Brown, "The Rise and Function of the Holy Man in Late Antiquity, *Journal of Roman Studies,* 61 (1971): 80–101; idem., "The Saint as Exemplar in Late Antiquity," in John Stratton Hawley, ed. *Saints and Virtues* (Berkeley: Univ. of California Press, 1987), 3–35.

34. Rachel Hosmer and Alan Jones, *Living in the Spirit* (New York: Seabury Press, 1979), 232.

35. John Caird, *An Introduction to the Philosophy of Religion* (1880), quoted in William James, *The Varieties of Religious Experience* (Cambridge, MA: Harvard Univ. Press, 1985), 356–57.

36. Priklonskii, 8.

37. Correspondence with Sister Macrina (now Mother Macaria) of New Valaam Monastery, Ouzinskie, Alaska, 27 March 1990.

38. See Valerie Saiving Goldstein, "The Human Situation: A Feminine Viewpoint," in Simon Doniger, ed. *The Nature of Man in Theological and Psychological Perspective* (Harper & Row, 1962), 151–70; Ann Belford Ulanov, *Receiving Woman: Studies in the Psychology and Theology of the Feminine* (Philadelphia: Westminster Press, 1981); and Wendy Wright, "The Feminine Dimensions of Contemplation," in Mary E. Giles, ed. *The Feminist Mystic. And Other Essays on Women and Spirituality* (New York: Crossroad, 1982), 103–19.

Chapter Three: Matrona Naumovna Popova

1. See Brenda Meehan-Waters, "From Contemplative Practice," 142–56.

2. The details of her life are taken from: Gerontii (ieromonakh), *Zhizn' Matrony Naumovny Popovoi. Osnovatel'nitsy pervogo strannopriimnogo doma v g. Zadonske,* 4th ed. (Voronezh, 1889). Gerontii, who later became a monk, was an orphan Matrona took care of as a youth.

3. On Melania's life, see Makariia, Bishop of Orlov, "Zhizneopisanie zatvornitsy Melanii," *Strannik,* vol. 1 (St. Petersburg, 1871), and Gerontii (ieromonakh), *Istoricheskoe opisanie Eletskogo znamenskogo devich'iago monastyria, chto na Kamennoi gore* (Elets, 1895), 47–49.

4. Gerontii, *Zhizn' Matrony Naumovny Popovoi*, 8.

5. Ibid., 9–10.

6. "Pilgrimages," *New Catholic Encyclopedia*, vol. 11 (New York: McGraw-Hill, 1967), 362.

7. Victor Turner and Edith Turner, *Image and Pilgrimage in Christian Culture. Anthropological Perspectives* (New York: Columbia Univ. Press, 1978), 6.

8. Ibid., 6–8.

9. Gromyko, 99–103.

10. See Michel Evdokimov, *Pèlerins russes et vagabonds mystiques* (Paris: Les éditions du cerf, 1987).

11. "Pilgrimages," *New Catholic Encyclopedia*, 368.

12. V. N. Andreev, *Zhizn' i deiatel'nost' Baronessy Rozen v monashestve igumenii Mitrofanii*, vol. 1 (St. Petersburg, 1876), 117.

13. Ibid., 11–12.

14. Ibid., 14.

15. "Matrona Naumovna Popova, osnovatel'nitsa pervago strannopriimnogo doma v gorode Zadonske," *Zhizneopisaniia otechestvennykh podvizhnikov blagochestiia 18 i 19 vekov*, vol. 8 of 12 vols. (Moscow, 1906–10), 353.

16. Ibid., 360.

17. Gerontii, 15; "Staritsa Matrona Naumovna (u. 17 avgusta 1851 g.) goroda Zadonska," *RPZhM*, 145.

18. "Matrona Naumovna Popova," *Zhizneopisanie*, 355; *RPZhM*, 145.

19. Gerontii, *Zhizn' Matrony Naumovny Popovoi*, 19, and throughout.

20. *RPZhM*, 146.

21. Ibid., 146–47; Gerontii, *Zhizn' Matrony Naumovny Popovoi*, 23.

22. *RPZhM*, 147.

23. *The Way of the Pilgrim and The Pilgrim Continues His Way*, trans. from the Russian by R. M. French (New York: Seabury Press, 1965).

24. Gerontii, *Zhizn' Matrony Naumovny Popovoi*, 30.

25. *Prayer Book* (Jordanville, NY: Holy Trinity Monastery, 1960), 290.

26. *RPZhM*, 147.

27. Ibid., 148.

28. "Matrona Naumovna Popova," *Zhizneopisaniia*, 362–63.

29. Ibid., 359.

30. Ibid., 367.

31. Gerontii, *Zhizn' Matrony Naumovny Popovoi*, 41.

32. Filaret (Drozdov), *Mneniia, otzyvy i pis'ma Filareta, mitropolita moskovskogo i kolomenskogo, po raznym voprosam za 1821–1867 gg.*, ed. L. Brodskii (Moscow, 1905), 160–61.

33. "Matrona Naumovna Popova," *Zhizneopisaniia*, 367.

34. Ibid., 364.

35. In the Orthodox church, the four great fasts include Great Lent (the forty days before Easter), the Lent of the Holy Apostles (June 16–28), St. Mary's Lent

(August 1–14), and the Lent preceding Christmas (November 15–December 24).

36. "Proekt pravil dliia upravleniia otkritoiu s Vysochaishago soizvoleniia Tikhonovskoiu zhenskoiu obshchinoiu s strannoprimym pri nei domom v gorode zadonske, odobrennykh Voronezhskim eparkhial'nym nachal'stvom i ne otmennykh Sv. Pr. Sinodom," in Gerontii, *Zhizn' Matrony Naumovny Popovoi*, 65–68.

37. Ibid., 67–68.

38. Filaret, *Mneniia*, 160–61; Gerontii, 65–68. In Denisov's comprehensive survey of the monastic institutions of Russia in 1907, he says that the Troitskii Tikhonovskii Zadonskii communal women's monastery was established in the 1830s by Matrona Naumovna Popova under the name of a Wayfarer's Home of Sisters of Mercy; officially recognized by the Synod in 1860 under the name Tikhonovskii Home of Sisters of Mercy; in 1880 given the name Tikhonovska-ia Community (*obshchina*); and in 1888 elevated to the status of a monastery (Denisov, 184).

39. John Shelton Curtiss, "Russian Sisters of Mercy in the Crimea, 1854–1855," *Slavic Review*, 35, no. 1 (March 1966): 84.

40. "Sestry i brat'ia miloserdiia," *Entsiklopedicheskii slovar'*, vol. 58 (St. Petersburg, 1900), 74.

41. On the criticism of monasticism, see *Igumeniia Feofaniia* (St. Petersburg, 1868), 30–31. On the question of the social role of the Orthodox church, see Simon Dixon, "The Church's Social Role in St. Petersburg, 1880–1914," in Geoffrey A. Hosking, ed. *Church, Nation and State*, 167–92.

42. "Sestry i brat'ia miloserdiia," 714.

43. Meehan-Waters, "From Contemplative Practice to Charitable Activity, 148.

44. Denisov, 184–85.

45. Gerontii, *Zhizn' Matrony Naumovny Popovoi*, 60.

46. See Denisov, which contains information on the charitable establishments of the 540 men's monasteries, 367 women's monasteries, and 61 women's communities (*obshchiny*) existing in Russia in 1907.

Chapter Four: Mother Angelina

1. S. N. Snessoreva, *Monakhinia Angelina (v mire Aleksandra Filippovna Fon-Roze) osnovatel'nitsa i stroitel'nitsa Sviato-Troitskoi Tvorozhkovskoi zhenskoi obshchiny vozvedennoi v monastyr' s naimenovaniem ego Sviato-Troitskim obshchezhitel'nym zhenskim monastyrem* (St. Petersburg, 1888), 3.

2. Isabel de Madariaga, *Russia in the Age of Catherine the Great* (New Haven and London: Yale Univ. Press, 1981), 493.

3. Snessoreva, 5–6.

4. Ibid., 7.

5. Ibid., 9.

6. Ibid., 7–9.

7. Ibid., 9.
8. Ibid., 11.
9. Ibid., 12.
10. Ibid., 12–13, 103.
11. Ibid., 14.
12. Ibid., 18–19.
13. Ibid., 19.
14. Ibid., 20–21.
15. Ibid., 24-28.
16. Ibid., 30.
17. Ibid., 151–52.
18. Tsentral'nyi gosudarstvennyi istoricheskii arkhiv Sankt Peterburga (hereafter TsGIA SPb), f. 19 (S-Peterburgskaia dukhovnaia konsistoriia), op. 113, d. 2947, "Vedomosti o nakhodiashchikhsia sestrakh v Sviato-Troitskoi Tvorozhkovskoi zhenskoi obshchin za 1877 god," l. 1 ob.-6.
19. *Zhenskie obshchiny*, and the monasteries that derived from them, were organized according to communal (cenobitic) rule and were called *obshchezhitel'nye*, in contrast to traditional men's and women's monasteries, which were noncommunal (*neobshchezhitel'nye*) and followed an idiorhythmic pattern. Rather than living in communal dormitories, nuns and novices in traditional monasteries lived in private cells, which they considered their own property. On entering the monastery, they would buy a cell from a previous occupant or build one of their own. In addition, each nun had responsibility for her own housekeeping tasks, food purchases, and preparation. When a refectory existed, it was most often frequented by the poorer nuns and novices, with the more well-to-do preferring to eat in their own cells. In this situation, there was little communal life or discipline; cloistering was impossible because of the need to shop in markets (and to sell one's handicrafts for self-support); and energy that could have been expended on spiritual edification, communal work, or charitable activity was dissipated on individual housekeeping tasks. See Brenda Meehan-Waters, "Metropolitan Filaret (Drozdov) and the Reform of Russian Women's Monastic Communities," *The Russian Review*, 50 (July 1991): 310–23.
20. Snessoreva, 31.
21. Ibid., 30–31, 36.
22. Ibid., 48–52.
23. Denisov, 752.
24. TsGIA SPb, f. 19, op. 113, d. 3828, ll.139-148.
25. TsGIA SPb, f. 19, op. 113, d. 4150, "Vedomosti i posluzhnye spiski monashestvuiushchikh za 1907 god," ll. 71-94. Denisov gives figures for 1907 of one abbess, thirteen nuns, one novice, and fifty-five *prozhivaiushchie na ispytanii*; he has no data on social origins (Denisov, 752).
26. Snessoreva, 102.

27. Ibid., 106.
28. TsGIA SPb, f. 19, op. 113, d. 2947, l.; d. 3828, l.
29. Meehan-Waters, "To Save Oneself," 127–29, and "Metropolitan Filaret," 18.
30. *Prayer Book,* rev. 4th ed. (Jordanville, NY: Holy Trinity Monastery, 1986), 265–315.
31. Snessoreva, 45.
32. *Prayer Book,* 4th ed., 294–95.
33. Ibid., 43, 39.
34. Ibid., 66–68.

Chapter Five: Abbess Taisiia

1. *Abbess Thaisia, the Autobiography of a Spiritual Daughter of St. John of Kronstadt* (Platina, CA: St. Herman of Alaska Brotherhood Press, 1989), 31.
2. Ibid., 33.
3. Ibid., 35.
4. Ibid., 36–37.
5. Ibid., 38.
6. Ibid., 39–42.
7. Ibid., 44.
8. Ibid., 39.
9. Ibid., 45.
10. Ibid., 49.
11. Ibid., 49–51.
12. Ibid., 52–53.
13. Ibid., 54.
14. Ibid., 57–58.
15. Ibid., 60.
16. Ibid., 64–65.
17. Ibid., 69.
18. Ibid., 73–82.
19. Ibid., 84.
20. Ibid., 87–88.
21. Ibid., 95.
22. Denisov, 611.
23. *Abbess Thaisia,* 82.
24. Ibid., 102–5.
25. Ibid., 103–4.
26. Ibid., 114–16.
27. Ibid., 109–11.
28. Ibid., 119–24.
29. Ibid., 125–28.
30. Ibid., 129–40.

31. Ibid., 141–43. On the Zverin convent, see Denisov, 599–600.
32. *Abbess Thaisia*, 161–63.
33. Ibid., 146.
34. Ibid., 147.
35. Ibid., 142.
36. Ibid., 158–60.
37. Ibid., 163. For the date of appointment, see "Modern Matericon: In Memory of Abbess Thaisia," *The Orthodox Word*, 146 (1989): 293. For the Zvanskii Znamenskii convent, see Denisov, 603.
38. *Abbess Thaisia*, 173–74.
39. "Modern Matericon," 293.
40. *Abbess Thaisia*, 171–74.
41. "The History of Abbess Thaisia's Leushino Convent," *The Orthodox Word*, 146 (1989): 161–63, 173–89; *Russkii Palomnik*, 11 (1895), no. 17: 257–59, no. 18: 280–85.
42. "History of . . . Leushino Convent," 161–62, 175–87.
43. *Abbess Thaisia*, 175.
44. Ibid., 175–76.
45. Ibid., 178–80.
46. Ibid., 181–87.
47. Ibid., 188.
48. Ibid., 188–90.
49. For an excellent introduction to St. John of Kronstadt, see W. Jardine Grisbrooke, ed. *The Spiritual Counsels of Father John of Kronstadt* (Crestwood, NY: St. Vladimir's Seminary Press, 1981).
50. *Abbess Thaisia*, 193.
51. Ibid., 194.
52. Ibid., 195–98.
53. Novgorod *Vedomosti*, 1915; "In Memory of Abbess Thaisia," *The Orthodox Word*, 148 (1989): 291; "Leushinskii Ioanno-Predtechenskii monastyr' i igumeniia Taisiia," in *Russkoe pravoslavnoe zhenskoe monashestvo*, 237.
54. Denisov, 612.
55. Denisov, 34–35, 711–12, 750; V. Georgievsky, "Abbess Thaisia's Contribution to Spiritual Literature," *The Orthodox Word*, 133 (1987): 118, translated from *Tserkovnie vedomosti* (St. Petersburg, 1915), no. 2, reprinted in *Abbess Thaisia*, 311–17.
56. Igumeniia Taisiia, Pis'ma k novonachal'noi inokine o glavneishikh obiazannostiakh inocheskoi zhizni. Sostavleno na osnovanii sviatootecheskikh asketicheskikh Pisanii, primerov Sv. Ottsev i mnogoletniago sobstvennogo opyta (St. Petersburg, 1900).
57. Abbot Herman, "Introduction to the Autobiography of Abbess Thaisia," *The Orthodox Word*, 133 (1987): 70.
58. Denisov, ix–xii.

59. Pis'ma k novonachal'noi inokine, 5–6.
60. Ibid., 10–12.
61. Ibid., 30–31.
62. In the Russian Psalter, this is Psalm 46; in the Western church, Psalm 47.
63. Pis'ma k novonachal'noi inokine, 24–28.
64. Ibid., 64–67.
65. Ibid., 74–75.
66. "Conversation Between St. John of Kronstadt and Abbess Thaisia," The Orthodox Word, 147 (1989): 210–11.
67. Ibid., 221–22.
68. Ibid., 148 (1989): 305–6.
69. Ibid., 147 (1989): 222–23.
70. Abbess Thaisia, 315.
71. Ibid., 316.
72. Ibid., 230.
73. Ibid., 229.
74. Ibid., 239–40.
75. Ibid., 234–35.
76. Ibid., 25.
77. Ibid., 25–26.
78. Carolyn C. Heilbrun, Writing a Woman's Life (New York: Ballantine Books, 1988), 12–23.
79. Ibid., 22–23. See also Patricia Spacks, "Selves in Hiding," in Estelle C. Jelinek, ed. Women's Autobiography (Bloomington: Indiana Univ. Press, 1980), 112–32.
80. On the importance of claiming the equal authority of women's experience, see Anne E. Carr, Transforming Grace: Christian Tradition and Women's Experience (San Francisco: Harper & Row, 1990), 141.
81. See for example, Mary Daly, The Church and the Second Sex (New York: Harper & Row, 1968), and Rosemary Radford Ruether, Religion and Sexism: Images of Women in the Jewish and Christian Traditions (New York: Simon & Schuster, 1974).
82. Abbess Thaisia, 26.
83. The Saint Herman Calendar (Platina, CA: St. Herman of Alaska Brotherhood, 1990), 9.

Conclusion

1. For a discussion of anorexic behavior and symptoms in medieval Italian women saints, see Rudolph M. Bell, Holy Anorexia (Chicago: Univ. of Chicago Press, 1985).
2. Andrew Sorokowski, "Church and State, 1917–1964" in Eugene B. Shirley, Jr., and Michael Rowe, eds. Candle in the Wind. Religion in the Soviet Union (Washington, DC: Ethics and Public Policy Center, 1989), 29–30. See also Glennys Jeanne Young, "Rural Religion and Soviet Power, 1921–1932," Ph.D. diss., Univ. of California, Berkeley, 1989.

3. Sorokowski, "Church and State," 35–40. Grace Swift, "Soviet Convents," *Review for Religious* (January–February 1986): 69–77.
4. Donald Weinstein and Rudolph M. Bell, *Saints and Society: The Two Worlds of Western Christendom, 1000–1700* (Chicago: Univ. of Chicago Press, 1982), 220–38.
5. Caroline Walker Bynum, *Holy Feast and Holy Fast. The Religious Significance of Food to Medieval Women* (Berkeley: Univ. of California Press, 1987), 25.
6. Gerald G. May, *The Awakened Heart. Living Beyond Addiction* (New York: Harper Collins, 1991), 193.
7. Gerald May, "Contemplative Frontiers Between Psychology and Spirituality," lecture delivered at Shalem Institute for Spiritual Formation, Washington, DC, 28 October 1991.
8. Evelyn Underhill, *The Spiritual Life* (Harrisburg, PA: Morehouse Publishing, 1955), 52–54.
9. Ibid., 54.
10. Carr, *Transforming Grace,* 186.

◆

Selected Bibliography

Russian Archival Sources

Tsentral'nyi gosudarstvennyi istoricheskii arkhiv Sankt Peterburga, f. 19
Rossiiskii gosudarstvennyi istoricheskii arkhiv, f. 796, f. 797
Tsentral'nyi gosudarstvennyi istoricheskii arkhiv goroda Moskvy, f. 203

Russian Published Sources

Andreev, V. N. *Zhizn' i deiatel'nost' Baronessy Rozen v monashestve igumenii Mitrofanii*. St. Petersburg, 1876.

Bol'shaia sovetskaia entsiklopediia, 3rd. ed., vol. 22. Moscow, 1975.

Bulgakov, S. V., comp. *Nastol'naia kniga dlia sviashchenno-tserkovno-sluzhitelei. Sbornik svedenii, kasaiushchikhsia preimuchchestvenno prakticheskoi deiatel'nosti otchestvennogo dukhovenstva*, 2nd ed. Khar'kov, 1900.

Denisov, L. V. *Pravoslavnye monastyri rossiiskoi imperii. Polnyi spisok vsekh 1105 nyne sushchestvuiushchikh v 75 guberniakh oblastiakh Rossii i 2 inostrannykh gosudarstvakh muzhiskikh, zhenskikh monastyrei, arkhiereiskikh domov i zhenskikh obshchin*. Moscow, 1908.

Dobrotvotrskii, N. "Krest'ianskie iuridicheskie obychai: Po materialam, sobrannym v vostochnoi chasti Vladimirskoi gubernii." In *Iuridicheskii vestnik*, 261–93. Moscow, 1889.

Filaret (Drozdov). *Mneniia, otzyvy i pis'ma Filareta, mitropolita moskovskogo i kolomenskogo, po raznym voprosam za 1821–1867 gg.*, ed. L. Brodskii. Moscow, 1905.

————. *Pis'ma mitropolita moskovskogo Filareta k namestniku sviatotroit-skiia sergievy lavry arkhimandritu Antoniiu, 1831–1867 gg.* Moscow, 1877–84.

————. *Pis'ma moskovskogo mitropolita Filareta k igumenii spasoborodin-skogo monastyria Sergii.* Tver, 1890.

Gerontii (ieromonakh). *Istoricheskoe opisanie Eletskogo znamenskogo de-vich'iago monastyria, chto na Kamennoi gore.* Elets, 1895.

————. *Zhizn' Matrony Naumovny Popovoi. Osnovatel'nitsy pervogo stranno-priimnogo doma v g. Zadonske,* 4th. ed. Voronezh, 1889.

Gromyko, M. M. *Traditsionnye normy povedeniia i formy obshcheniia russkikh krest'ian XIX v.* Moscow: Nauka, 1986.

Igumeniia Feofaniia. St. Petersburg, 1868.

Makariia, Bishop of Orlov. "Zhizneopisanie zatvornitsy Melanii." In *Stran-nik,* vol. 1. St. Petersburg, 1871.

"Matrona Naumovna Popova, osnovatel'nitsa pervago strannopriimnogo doma v gorode Zadonske." In *Zhizneopisaniia otechestvennykh podvizh-nikov blagochestiia 18 i 19 vekov,* vol. 8. Moscow, 1906–10.

"Monashestvo." In *Entsiklopedicheskii slovar',* vol. 38. St Petersburg, 1896.

"Pamiati pustynnozhitel'nitsy Anastasii Semenovny Logachevoi (inokini Afanasii)." In *Zhizneopisaniia otechestvennykh podvizhnikov blagochestiia 18 i 19 vekom,* vol. 2. Moscow, 1907. *Dopolnenie,* pt. 2. Moscow, 1916.

Priklonskii, Aleksandr. *Zhizn' pustynnitsy Anastasii Semenovny Logachevoi, vposledstvii monakhinia Afanasii, i vozniknovenia na meste eia podvigov zhenskoi obshchiny.* Moscow, 1902.

"Pustynitsa Anastasiia Semenovna Logacheva, vposledstvii monakhinia Afanasiia." In *Zhizneopisaniia otechestvennykh podvizhnikov blagochestiia 18 i 19 vekom,* vol. 2. Moscow, 1907.

Rashin, A. G. *Naselenie Rossii za 100 let.* Moscow, 1956.

"Sestry i brat'ia miloserdiia." In *Entsiklopedicheskii slovar',* vol. 58. St. Pe-tersburg, 1900.

Smirnov, S. A. "Missionerskaia deiatel'nost' tserkvi (Vtoraia polovina XIX v.–1917 g.)." In *Russkoe pravoslavie: vekhi istorii,* ed. A. I. Klibanov, 438–61. Moscow, 1989.

Snessoreva, S. N. *Monakhinia Angelina (v mire Aleksandra Filippova Fon-Roze) osnovatel'nitsa i stroitel'nitsa Sviato-Troitskoi Tvorozhkovskoi*

*zhenskoi obshchiny vozvedennoi v monastyr' s naimenovaniem ego Svi-
ato-Troitskim obshchezhitel'nym zhenskim monastyrem.* St. Petersburg,
1888.

Taisiia, comp. *Russkoe pravoslavnoe zhenskoe monashestvo XVIII–XX.* Jordanville, NY: Holy Trinity Monastery, 1985.

Taisiia, Ig. *Pis'ma k novonachal'noi inokine o glavneishikh obiazannostiakh inocheskoi zhizni. Sostavleno na osnovanii sviatootecheskikh asketicheskikh
Pisanii, prierov Sv. Ottsev i mnogoletnogo sobstvennogo opyta.* St. Petersburg, 1909.

Tokmakov, I. F. *Istoricheskoe opisanie moskovskogo novodeviich'iago
monastyria.* Moscow, 1885.

Tolycheva, T. (E. V. Novosil'tseva). *Spaso-Borodinskii monastyr' i ego osnovatel'nitsa. Posviashchaetsia vsem pochitaiushchim pamiat' Margarity
Mikhailovny Tuchkovoi,* 3rd. ed. Moscow, 1889.

Tul'tseva, L. A. "Chernichki," in *Nauka i religiia,* 11 (1970): 80–82.

Zhizneopisaniia otechestvennykh podvizhnikov blagochestiia 18 i 19 vekov, 12
vols. Moscow, 1906–10.

Zverinskii, V. V. *Material dlia istoriko-topograficheskogo issledovaniia o
pravoslavnykh monastyriakh v rossiiskoi imperii.* 2 vols. St. Petersburg, 1890.

Western Language Sources

*Abbess Thaisia, the Autobiography of a Spiritual Daughter of St. John of Kron-
stadt.* Platina, CA: St. Herman of Alaska Brotherhood Press, 1989.

Allchin, A. M. *The Silent Rebellion. Anglican Religious Communities,
1845–1900.* London: SCM Press, 1958.

Arseniev, Nicholas. *Russian Piety.* New York: St. Vladimir's Press, 1964.

Bell, Rudolph M. *Holy Anorexia.* Chicago: Univ. of Chicago Press, 1985.

Bolshakoff, Sergius. *Russian Mystics.* Kalamazoo, MI: Cistercian Publications, 1976.

Book of Common Prayer. New York: Church Hymnal Corp., 1979.

Brock, Sebastian P., and Susan Ashbrook Harvey. *Holy Women of the Syrian
Orient.* Berkeley: Univ. of California Press, 1987.

Brown, Peter. "The Rise and Function of the Holy Man in Late Antiquity."
In *Journal of Roman Studies,* 61 (1971): 80–101.

◆ Selected Bibliography ◆

————. "The Saint as Exemplar in Late Antiquity." In *Saints and Virtues*, ed. John Stratton Hawley, 3–15. Berkeley: Univ. of California Press, 1987.

Bynum, Caroline Walker. *Holy Feast and Holy Fast. The Religious Significance of Food to Medieval Women*. Berkeley: Univ. of California Press, 1987.

Carr, Anne E. *Transforming Grace: Christian Tradition and Women's Experience*. San Francisco: Harper & Row, 1990.

Campbell, Mary B. *The Witness and the Other World. Exotic European Travel Writing, 400–1600*. Ithaca: Cornell Univ. Press, 1988.

Claus, Claire Louise. "Die Russischen Frauenklöster um die Wende des 18. Jahrhunderts, Ihre Karitative Tätigkeit und Religiöse Bedeutung." In *Kirche im Osten* (Amsterdam, 1969), band 4 (1961): 37–60.

Coleman, John A. "Conclusion: After Sainthood?" In *Saints and Virtues*, ed. John Stratton Hawley, 205–25. Berkeley: Univ. of California Press, 1987.

Collins, David M. "The Role of the Orthodox Missionary in the Altai: Archimandrite Makarii and V. I. Verbitskii." In *Church, Nation and State in Russia and Ukraine*, ed. Geoffrey A. Hosking, 96–107. London: Macmillan, 1991.

"Conversations Between St. John of Kronstadt and Abbess Thaisia." In *The Orthodox Word*, 147 (1989): 209–30, 148 (1989): 305–16, 323–35.

Cracraft, James. *The Church Reform of Peter the Great*. London: Macmillan, 1971.

Curtiss, John Shelton. "Russian Sisters of Mercy in the Crimea, 1854–1855." In *Slavic Review*, 35 (March 1966): 84–100.

Daly, Mary. *The Church and the Second Sex*. New York: Harper & Row, 1968.

Davis, Bruce. *Monastery Without Walls. Daily Life in the Silence*. Berkeley: Celestial Arts, 1990.

Dixon, Simon. "The Church's Social Role in St. Petersburg, 1880–1914." In *Church, Nation and State in Russia and Ukraine*, ed. Geoffrey A. Hosking,167–92. London: Macmillan, 1992.

Edwards, David W. "The System of Nicholas I in Church-State Relations." In *Russian Orthodoxy Under the Old Regime*, ed. Robert L. Nichols and Theofanis Stavrou, 154–69. Minneapolis: Univ. of Minnesota, 1978.

Edwards, Tilden. *Living Simply Through the Day. Spiritual Survival in a Complex Age*. New York: Paulist Press, 1977.

◆ *Selected Bibliography* ◆

Evdokimov, Michel. *Pèlerins russes et vagabonds mystiques*. Paris: Les éditions du cerf, 1987.

Foster, Richard J. *Celebration of Discipline. The Path to Spiritual Growth*. San Francisco: Harper & Row, 1988.

Freeze, Gregory L. *The Parish Clergy in Nineteenth-Century Russia. Crisis, Reform, Counter-Reform*. Princeton: Princeton Univ. Press, 1983.

Georgievsky, V. "Abbess Thaisia's Contribution to Spiritual Literature." In *The Orthodox Word*, 133 (1987): 114–19.

Glickman, Rose. *Russian Factory Women. Workplace and Society, 1880–1914*. Berkeley: Univ. of California Press, 1984.

Goldstein, Valerie Saiving. "The Human Situation: A Feminine Viewpoint." In *The Nature of Man in Theological and Psychological Perspective*, ed. Simon Doniger, 151–70. San Francisco: Harper & Row, 1962.

Great Soviet Encyclopedia. A Translation of the Third Edition, vol. 22. New York: Macmillan, 1979.

Greene, Dana. *Evelyn Underhill. Artist of the Infinite Life*. New York: Crossroad, 1990.

Grisbrooke, W. Jardine, ed. *Spiritual Counsels of Father John of Kronstadt*. Crestwood, NY: St. Vladimir's Seminary Press, 1981.

Harvey, Susan Ashbrook. *Asceticism and Society in Crisis. John of Ephesus and the Lives of the Eastern Saints*. Berkeley: Univ. of California Press, 1990.

Heilbrun, Carolyn C. *Writing a Woman's Life*. New York: Ballantine Books, 1988.

Herman, Abbot. "Modern Matericon: Abbess Thaisia. Introduction." In *The Orthodox Word*, 133 (1987): 69-71.

Heyward, Carter. *Touching Our Strength. The Erotic as Power and the Love of God*. San Francisco: HarperSanFrancisco, 1989.

"History of Abbess Thaisia's Leushino Convent." In *The Orthodox Word*, 146 (1989): 161–62, 175–89.

Hosmer, Rachel, and Alan Jones. *Living in the Spirit*. New York: Seabury Press, 1979.

"In Memory of Abbess Thaisia." In *The Orthodox Word*, 148 (1989): 288–303.

James, William. *The Varieties of Religious Experience*. Cambridge, MA: Harvard Univ. Press, 1985.

Leech, Kenneth. *Soul Friend. The Practice of Christian Spirituality*. San Francisco: Harper & Row, 1980.

Little Russian Philokalia. Vol. 1: St. Seraphim. Platina, CA.: St. Herman of Alaska Brotherhood, 1980.

McNamara, JoAnn. *A New Song: Celibate Women in the First Three Christian Centuries*. New York: Haworth Press, 1983.

Madariaga, Isabel de. *Russia in the Age of Catherine the Great*. New Haven and London: Yale Univ. Press, 1981.

May, Gerald G. *The Awakened Heart. Living Beyond Addiction*. New York: HarperCollins, 1991.

Meehan-Waters, Brenda. "The Authority of Holiness: Women Ascetics and Spiritual Elders in Nineteenth-Century Russia." In *Church, Nation and State in Russia and Ukraine*, ed. Geoffrey A. Hosking, 38–51. London: Macmillan, 1991.

———. "From Contemplative Practice to Charitable Activity: Russian Women's Religious Communities and the Development of Charitable Work." In *Lady Bountiful Revisited: Women, Philanthropy, and Power*, ed. Kathleen McCarthy, 142–56. New Brunswick, NJ: Rutgers Univ. Press, 1990.

———. "Metropolitan Filaret (Drozdov) and the Reform of Russian Women's Monastic Communities." In *Russian Review*, 50 (1991): 310–23.

———. "Popular Piety, Local Initiative and the Founding of Women's Religious Communities in Russia, 1764– 1917." In *St. Vladimir's Theological Quarterly*, 25 (1986): 117–42. Reprinted in *Seeking God: The Recovery of Religious Identity in Orthodox Russia, Ukraine and Georgia*, ed. Stephen K. Batalden. DeKalb: Northern Illinois Univ. Press, forthcoming 1993.

———. "To Save Oneself: Russian Peasant Women and the Development of Women's Religious Communities in Pre-Revolutionary Russia." In *Russian Peasant Women*, ed. Beatrice Farnsworth and Lynne Viola, 121–33. New York: Oxford Univ. Press, 1992.

New Catholic Encyclopedia, ed. S. V. "Pilgrimages." 1967.

New Encyclopedia Britannica. Micropedia, vol. 2, 1978 ed.

New English Bible with the Apocrypha. Oxford Study Edition. New York: Oxford Univ. Press, 1976.

Prayer Book. Jordanville, NY: Holy Trinity Monastery, 1960, and rev. 4th ed., 1986.

Priklonsky, Fr. Alexander. Blessed Athanasia. Disciple of St. Seraphim. Platina, CA.: St. Herman of Alaska Brotherhood, 1980.

Ruether, Rosemary Radford. Religion and Sexism: Images of Women in the Jewish and Christian Traditions. New York: Simon & Schuster, 1974.

Saint Herman Calendar. Platina, CA: St. Herman of Alaska Brotherhood, 1990.

Senyk, Sophia. Women's Monasteries in Ukraine and Belorussia to the Period of Suppressions. Vol. 222: Orientalia Christiana Analecta. Rome: Pont. Institutum Studiorum Orientalium, 1983.

Service Book of the Holy Orthodox-Catholic Apostolic Church, comp. and trans. Isabel Hapgood, 3rd. ed. New York: Syrian Antiochian Orthodox Archdiocese of New York and All North America, 1956.

Smolitsch, Igor. Geschichte der Russischen Kirche, 1700–1917. Leiden: E. J. Brill, 1964.

Sorokowski, Andrew. "Church and State, 1917–1964." In Candle in the Wind. Religion in the Soviet Union, ed. Eugene B. Shirley, Jr., and Michael Rowe, 21–64. Washington, DC: Ethics and Public Policy Center, 1989.

Spacks, Patricia. "Selves in Hiding." In Women's Autobiography, ed. Estelle C. Jelinek, 112–32. Bloomington: Indiana Univ. Press, 1980.

Swift, Grace. "Soviet Convents." In Review for Religious, (January–February 1986): 69–77.

Thomas, Marie. "Muscovite Convents in the 17th Century." In Russian History, 10 (1983): 230–42.

Turner, Victor, and Edith Turner. Image and Pilgrimage in Christian Culture. Anthropological Perspectives. New York: Columbia Univ. Press, 1978.

Ulanov, Ann Belford. Receiving Woman: Studies in the Psychology and Theology of the Feminine. Philadelphia: Westminster Press, 1981.

Underhill, Evelyn. The Spiritual Life. Harrisburg, PA: Morehouse Publishing, 1955.

The Way of the Pilgrim and The Pilgrim Continues His Way, trans. R. M. French. New York: Seabury Press, 1965.

Weinstein, Donald, and Rudolph M. Bell. *Saints and Society: The Two Worlds of Western Christendom, 1000-1700.* Chicago: Univ. of Chicago Press, 1982.

Wright, Wendy. "The Feminine Dimensions of Contemplation." In *The Feminist Mystic. And Other Essays on Women and Spirituality*, ed. Mary E. Giles, 103–19. New York: Crossroads, 1982.

Young, Glennys Jeanne. "Rural Religion and Soviet Power, 1921–1932." Ph.D. diss., Univ. of California, Berkeley, 1989.

Index

◆ *Index* ◆

Dress, monastic, 88, 89
Dying, 69

Edwards, Tilden, 8
1812 Overture (Tchaikovsky), 19
Elders. *See Starets/Staritsa*
Empowerment. *See* Women

Faith, 135
Fasts, Orthodox, 160–61n.35
Feminism, 95, 140–41, 151
Feodosii, Abbot, 139
Feokfista, Mother, 111–12, 114, 131
Filaret, Metropolitan: Margarita and, 21, 24, 25, 30–31, 34–35, 37, 38; and
  Tikhon-Zadonsk community, 72–73, 75, 76
Finances: charity, 68–69, 71; community, 12, 13, 28–32, 54–55, 89, 91, 107–10,
  121, 150; community building projects, 84–85, 90–91, 127; government reli-
  gious, 11–12, 13, 150; noncommunal monastic, 12, 113; women's monastic,
  12, 13, 31–32, 107–8, 109–10, 113. *See also* Poor
Fon-Roze, Karl Andreevich (Nikolai), 80–83, 94
Foster, Richard, 8

Gender differences, 144, 145–46; angelic life, 59–60; and compassion/contempla-
  tion, 78; family responsibilities, 45, 145; psalm readers, 46; in symbols,
  140–41. *See also* Men; Women
Generosity, 37, 53. *See also* Charitable work
Gerontii, 65, 67
Goldman, Emma, 140
Golovina, Anna Gavrilovna, 38–39
Government: Nicholas I, 28; and religion, 11–12, 13, 28–29, 54, 143–44, 150
Greene, Dana, 49
Grief, 24–25, 81, 144
Grigorii, Metropolitan, 85, 86
Guides. *See* Spiritual guides

Heilbrun, Carolyn, 95, 139–40
Hermits, 34, 42–45, 46–52, 58, 62, 156n.42
Holiness, 3, 4, 6, 143–51; of Anastasiia, 40, 56–58, 60, 149; of Angelina, 93–94,
  149; as fullness of being, 60, 151; of Magarita, 37–38, 144, 149; of Matrona,
  68–71, 77–78, 149; of Taisiia, 137–38, 149. *See also* Compassion; Contemplation; Discipline; Generosity; Humility; Love
Holy Synod, 11; book publishing by, 128; community elevated to monastery status
  by, 30–32, 126; pectoral cross from, 137; women's communities sanctioned by,

177